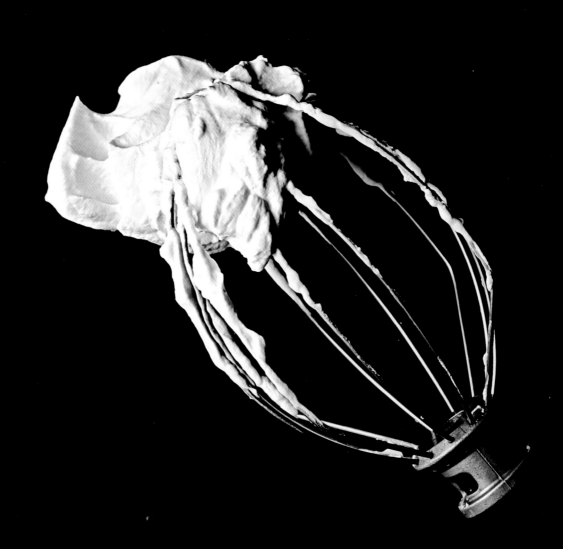

COMFORT
FOOD

RICK RODGERS

PHOTOGRAPHS BY
PEDEN+MUNK

weldonowen

WHAT IS COMFORT FOOD?

How do you even begin to define comfort food? It means something different to every one of us. It conjures up memories of childhood and makes us nostalgic for the more relaxed times of our youth. It is both nurturing and decadent, feeding our souls and encouraging an indulgent streak. It lifts our spirits when we are down and nourishes us when we are happy, soothing and satisfying us, like wrapping us in a big, warm quilt. Comfort foods are the cherished recipes, passed down through generations, that were served at the family table.

Even though everyone's roll call of ultimate comfort foods will differ, certain dishes turn up on nearly every list. These are the recipes I have gathered here. Some of the dishes reflect an earlier time when slow-simmered foods were daily occurrences, rather than a treat reserved for weekends. Others are easy to prepare whenever the mood strikes. For every recipe, I've tried to provide the ultimate, over-the-top version, using the best ingredients possible. It might not be the exact dish you remember from childhood, but it is guaranteed to taste great, and in many cases may even exceed your expectations.

In this collection, I've concentrated on lunch and dinner, the main meals of the day where cooks are most often hungry for a heaping serving of nostalgia. You'll find down-home American cooking, like grilled cheese sandwiches and tomato soup, and crispy fried chicken, as well as dishes borrowed from beyond our borders, such as French onion soup, lasagna Bolognese, and cheesy chicken enchiladas. Simply put, there is something here for all of us who take pleasure in sitting down to a table laden with comfort food.

—Rick Rodgers

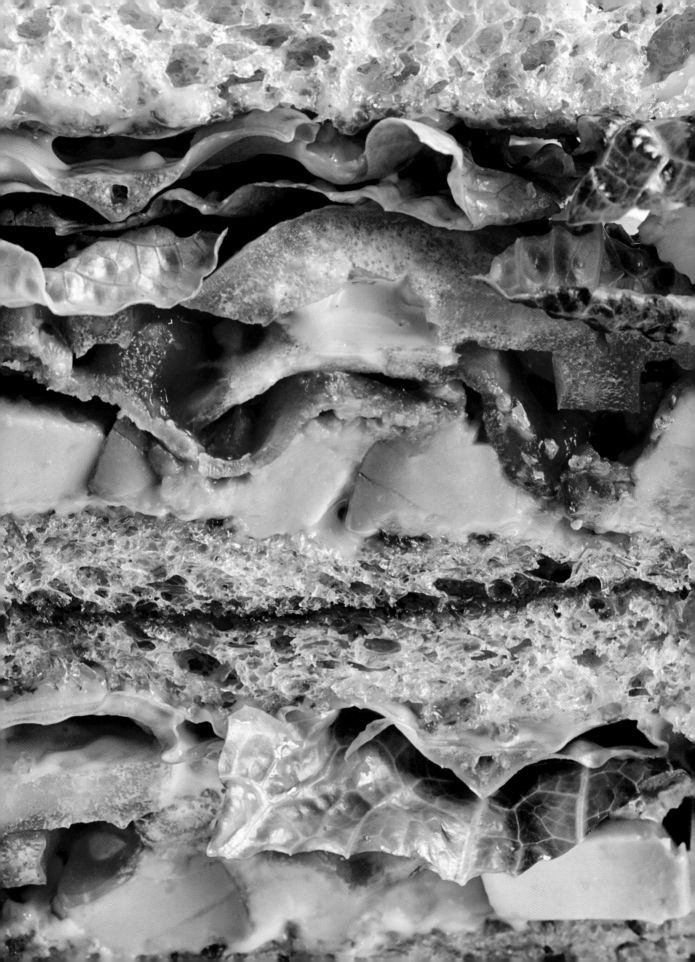

⚘LUNCH⚘

Chicken Caesar Salad 13

Tomato & Mozzarella
Salad with Pesto 14

Warm Spinach & Bacon Salad 16

Crab Louis 17

Savory Bread Salad 19

The Cobb 20

Cheesesteaks 22

Meatball Hoagies 23

Egg Salad Sandwiches 24

Tuna Melts 25

Lobster Rolls 27

Fried Chicken Sandwiches 28

Fried Oyster Po'Boys 29

BLTA Sandwiches 30

Crab Cakes with Lemon Aioli 32

Reuben Sandwiches 33

Ham & Gruyére
Croque Madame 35

Roasted Vegetable
& Goat Cheese Panini 36

Grilled Cheddar Sandwiches
with Bacon & Tomato 37

Grilled Panini with
Prosciutto & Mozzarella 38

Grilled PB & Chocolate
Sandwiches 40

Ricotta & Spinach Calzone 41

Grilled Cheese with Creamy
Tomato Soup 43

French Onion Soup 44

Broccoli & Cheddar Soup 47

Italian Bean & Pasta Soup 48

Clam Chowder 49

Chicken Noodle Soup 50

Classic Chicken Hash 52

Split Pea & Ham Hock
Soup 53

White Chicken &
Cannellini Chili 55

Vegetable, Corn
& Black Bean Chili 56

Black Bean & Chorizo Burritos 58

Roasted Red Pepper Frittata
with Sausage & Feta 59

Broccoli-Cheddar Quiche 61

One of the most beloved salads, Caesar has changed quite a bit from its roots at a Tijuana restaurant, used as a dip for romaine lettuce. The original dressing included a very softly boiled (coddled) egg, but this version gets its body and creaminess from Parmesan cheese.

CHICKEN CAESAR SALAD

Makes 4 servings

Extra-virgin olive oil, ¾ cup (6 fl oz/180 ml) plus 1 tablespoon

Parmesan cheese, ½ cup (2 oz/60 g) freshly grated plus a 4-ounce (125-g) wedge

Fresh lemon juice, ¼ cup (2 fl oz/60 ml)

Anchovy fillets in oil or anchovy paste, 1 teaspoon minced, drained

Garlic, 1 clove, peeled

Kosher salt and freshly ground pepper

Chicken breasts, 3 (about 6 ounces/185 g each), skinless and boneless, halved

Romaine hearts, 2

Parmesan Toast (page 75), chopped (optional)

To make the dressing, in a blender, process the ¾ cup (6 fl oz/180 ml) oil, the grated Parmesan, the lemon juice, anchovies, garlic, ½ teaspoon salt, and ½ teaspoon pepper to make a smooth, thick, dressing.

To cook the chicken, using a meat pounder, pound the chicken breasts until they are a uniform ½ inch (12 mm) thick. Sprinkle the chicken evenly with 1½ teaspoons salt and ½ teaspoon pepper.

In a large nonstick frying pan, heat the remaining 1 tablespoon oil over medium-high heat. Reduce the heat to medium. In batches to avoid crowding, add the chicken and cook until the underside is golden brown, about 4 minutes. Flip the chicken and continue cooking until the other side is golden brown and the chicken feels firm when pressed on top in the center, about 4 minutes more. Transfer to a carving board and let cool for 5 minutes. (If you wish, let the chicken cool completely. Wrap it in plastic wrap and refrigerate until chilled, at least 1 hour and up to 8 hours.) Slice the chicken across the grain into ½-inch (12-mm) thick slices.

Chop the romaine lengthwise or tear into bite-size pieces. In a large bowl, toss the romaine with the dressing. Season with salt and pepper to taste. Divide the salad among 4 bowls. Top each with equal amounts of the chicken slices and the Parmesan Toast. Using a swivel vegetable peeler, shave curls of cheese from the Parmesan wedge over the salad and serve at once.

Change it up Asiago or Grana Padano are good substitutes for the Parmesan, but don't use Romano, which is too sharp. Instead of chicken, top each serving with cooked shrimp or sliced steak. Add a tart bite with 1 cup (6 oz/190 g) halved cherry tomatoes.

This light salad is best served in the summer, when tomatoes are at the peak of their season. Grilled chicken or cooked and cooled grains, such as farro or couscous, transform this salad into a balanced meal.

TOMATO & MOZZARELLA SALAD WITH PESTO

Makes 4 servings

Basil Pesto (page 215 or purchased), 3 tablespoons

Red wine vinegar, 1½ tablespoons

Extra-virgin olive oil, ¼ cup (2 fl oz/60 ml)

Kosher salt and freshly ground pepper

Mixed red, yellow, and orange cherry tomatoes, about 4 cups (24 oz/750 g)

Fresh mozzarella, such as burrata, ciliegine, or bocconcino, ½ pound (250 g), torn or left whole

In a bowl, whisk together the pesto and vinegar. Whisking constantly, slowly add the oil until emulsified. Season to taste with salt and pepper.

Slice the tomatoes in half and add them and the mozzarella to the bowl, and toss gently. Season with salt and pepper and mound on a serving platter. Serve at once.

Change it up Tomatoes, mozzarella, and pesto are a classic panini combination. Instead of cherry tomatoes and mozzarella balls, use heirloom tomato slices and thinly sliced fresh mozzarella. On 1 slice sourdough bread, spread the pesto vinaigrette, then layer mozzarella slices, tomato slices, and more mozzarella slices, in that order. Spread a second bread slice with more pesto vinaigrette and place, pesto side down, onto the mozzarella. Brush the outside of the bread with olive oil. Using a panini grill, toast the sandwich until the bread is browned and the cheese is melted.

Smoky, salty bacon makes almost everything taste better, and this hearty salad is no exception. It may even make kids happily eat their greens. Bacon has lots of presence here, so look for good-quality, thick-cut bacon for the tastiest results. And try not to eat all the crisp bacon bits while you assemble the salads.

WARM SPINACH & BACON SALAD

Makes 6-8 servings

Extra-virgin olive oil, ½ cup (4 fl oz/125 ml)

Button mushrooms, 1 pound (500 g), halved

Fresh lemon juice, 1½ tablespoons

Garlic, 2 cloves, thinly sliced

Fresh thyme, 1 teaspoon minced

Red pepper flakes, ¼ teaspoon

Kosher salt and freshly ground pepper

Large eggs, 3

Baby spinach, 10 ounces (315 g)

Applewood-smoked bacon, 8 thick slices

Balsamic vinegar, 3 tablespoons

Whole-grain mustard, 1 tablespoon

Red onion, 1 small, thinly sliced

Cherry tomatoes, 1½ cups (9 oz/275 g), halved

In a frying pan, heat 2 tablespoons of the oil over medium-high heat. Add the mushrooms and cook, stirring occasionally, until they give off their juices and are lightly browned, 5–6 minutes. Transfer to a bowl. Add 4 tablespoons (2 fl oz/60 ml) of the oil, the lemon juice, garlic, thyme, and red pepper flakes, season with salt and pepper, and toss to coat. Let marinate for at least 1 hour or up to 24 hours.

To hard-boil the eggs, place them in a saucepan just large enough to hold them. Add cold water to cover by 1 inch (2.5 cm) and bring just to a boil over high heat. Remove the pan from the heat and cover. Let stand for 15 minutes. Drain the eggs, then transfer to a bowl of ice water and let cool. Peel and coarsely chop the eggs.

Put the spinach in a large bowl. Chop the bacon. In a large frying pan, fry the bacon over medium heat, stirring occasionally, until crisp and browned, about 7 minutes. Using a slotted spoon, transfer to paper towels to drain. Pour off all but 2 tablespoons of the fat in the pan. Off the heat, whisk the vinegar and mustard into the fat in the pan, then whisk in the remaining 2 tablespoons oil. Season to taste with salt and pepper and drizzle over the spinach. Toss to coat well.

Divide the dressed spinach among individual plates, top with the onion slices, tomatoes, marinated mushrooms, and chopped eggs. Sprinkle with the chopped bacon and serve at once.

Change it up You can top each serving with a poached egg instead of chopped hard-boiled egg. The fruity flavor of cider vinegar in place of the balsamic vinegar pairs nicely with the smoky bacon.

A Louis (pronounced LOO-ee) is traditionally served with just a few basic fresh vegetables, so as not to detract from the mound of fresh, sweet crabmeat. For a healthier, modernized spin, make this crab salad with a low-fat mayonnaise and serve atop a bed of fresh spinach.

CRAB LOUIS

Makes 4-6 servings

Large eggs, 4

Mayonnaise (page 216 or purchased), 1 cup (8 fl oz/250 ml)

Ketchup-style chili sauce, ¼ cup (2 fl oz/60 g)

Green bell pepper, 2 tablespoons minced

Green onions, 2, white and green parts, minced

Fresh lemon juice, 1 tablespoon

Iceberg lettuce, ½ head

Romaine lettuce hearts, 2

Fresh-cooked lump crabmeat, 1 pound (500 g)

Cherry tomatoes, ½ cup (3 oz/90 g), halved

English cucumber, ¼, thinly sliced

Lemon, 1, cut into wedges

To hard-boil the eggs, place them in a saucepan just large enough to hold them. Add cold water to cover by 1 inch (2.5 cm) and bring just to a boil over high heat. Remove the pan from the heat and cover. Let stand for 15 minutes. Drain the eggs, then transfer to a bowl of ice water and let cool. Peel the eggs and cut into quarters.

To make the dressing, in a small bowl, whisk together the mayonnaise, chili sauce, bell pepper, green onions, and lemon juice. Cover and refrigerate until serving.

Tear the iceberg lettuce into bite-sized pieces, and coarsely chop the romaine hearts. In a large bowl, toss together the lettuces. Distribute the lettuces in a thick layer on a large platter or divide evenly among 4–6 individual plates. Pick over the crabmeat for shell shards and cartilage. Heap the crabmeat down the center of the lettuce.

Arrange the tomatoes, cucumbers, and quartered eggs around the crab. Garnish with the lemon wedges and serve, passing the dressing on the side.

Change it up A Louis salad is often made with shrimp instead of crab, or with a combination of crab and shrimp. Use cooked, peeled, and deveined shrimp in the size you prefer (on the West Coast, tiny bay shrimp are usually the first choice). You can also top the salad with lightly cooked asparagus.

Although this salad has plenty of arugula, what makes it stand out at the table is the interplay of the toasted bread, crunchy pine nuts, and slightly chewy pancetta. The vinaigrette is made special by sautéing the shallots, which helps distribute their flavor throughout the salad.

SAVORY BREAD SALAD

Makes 4 servings

Pain au levain or country sourdough, 2 cups (4 oz/120 g) cubed

Olive oil, ½ cup (4 fl oz/125 ml) plus 3 tablespoons

Pine nuts, ⅓ cup (1 ¾ oz/50 g)

Pancetta, ¼ pound (125 g), chopped

Shallots, 2 tablespoons minced

Red wine vinegar, 2 tablespoons

Kosher salt and freshly ground pepper

Baby arugula, 6 ounces (185 g)

Preheat the oven to 350°F (180°C). Spread the bread cubes on a rimmed baking sheet and drizzle with 2 tablespoons of the oil. Bake until the bread is toasted but still slightly chewy, about 8 minutes. Let cool.

In a frying pan over medium-low heat, toast the pine nuts until golden, stirring continuously, about 5 minutes. Remove from the pan and set aside. In the same frying pan, combine the pancetta and 1 tablespoon of the oil over medium heat and cook, stirring occasionally, until the pancetta is browned and crisp, about 8 minutes. Using a slotted spoon, transfer to paper towels to drain. Pour off all but 1 tablespoon of the fat from the pan. Let the pan cool slightly.

Return the pan to medium heat, add the shallots, and cook, stirring frequently, until softened, about 2 minutes. Transfer to a small bowl and let cool. Add the vinegar to the cooled shallots, then slowly whisk in the ½ cup olive oil until well blended to make a vinaigrette. Season with salt and pepper.

In a large serving bowl, toss together the toasted bread cubes, arugula, toasted pine nuts, and pancetta. Add the vinaigrette and toss to coat evenly. Season with salt and pepper and serve at once.

Lighten it up For an entirely different but equally delicious bread salad, substitute toasted sliced almonds for the pine nuts, watercress for the arugula, and orange segments for the pancetta. Serve with a roasted chicken to transform this salad into a hearty meal.

Once little known outside of Hollywood, where it was a star of the Brown Derby restaurant menu, Cobb salad is now served everywhere. Heaped with blue cheese, bacon, chicken, and avocado, this hearty salad guarantees you won't be hungry until supper time. For a lighter meal, halve the amount of cheese and dressing used.

THE COBB

Makes 4 servings

Large eggs, 2

White wine vinegar, ¼ cup (2 fl oz/60 ml)

Dijon mustard, 1 teaspoon

Garlic, 1 clove, crushed

Extra-virgin olive oil, ¾ cup (6 fl oz/180 ml) plus 1 tablespoon

Kosher salt and freshly ground pepper

Skinless, boneless chicken breast halves, 3 (about 6 oz/185 g each)

Fresh flat-leaf parsley, 2 tablespoons minced

Fresh thyme, 2 teaspoons minced

Applewood-smoked bacon, 4 thick slices, chopped

Avocado, 1

Romaine lettuce hearts, 2, chopped

Cherry tomatoes, 2 cups (12 oz/375 g), halved

Gorgonzola or other mild blue cheese, 1 cup (5 oz/155 g) crumbled

To hard-boil the eggs, place them in a saucepan just large enough to hold them. Add cold water to cover by 1 inch (2.5 cm) and bring just to a boil over high heat. Remove the pan from the heat and cover. Let stand for 15 minutes. Drain the eggs, then transfer to a bowl of ice water and let cool. Peel the eggs and cut into quarters.

To make the vinaigrette, in a blender, combine the vinegar, mustard, and garlic. With the blender running, slowly add the ¾ cup (6 fl oz/180 ml) oil through the vent in the lid, processing until a thick dressing forms. Season with salt and pepper. Pour the dressing into a serving bowl.

Using a meat pounder, pound the chicken breasts until they are a uniform ½ inch (12 mm) thick. Season them with salt and pepper. Mix together the parsley and thyme, and sprinkle evenly over both sides of the breasts, pressing the herbs to help them adhere. In a large nonstick frying pan, heat the remaining 1 tablespoon oil over medium heat. Add the chicken and cook until the undersides are browned, about 5 minutes. Turn and cook until the second sides are browned and the breasts are opaque throughout, about 5 minutes more. Transfer to a plate and let cool.

Add the bacon to the frying pan and fry, stirring occasionally, until crisp and browned, about 4 minutes. Using a slotted spoon, transfer to paper towels to drain.

When ready to serve, slice the chicken breasts across the grain into strips. Halve, pit, peel, and cube the avocado. Divide the lettuce evenly among 4 individual plates, or heap it onto a platter. Arrange the chicken, bacon, tomatoes, avocado, eggs, and Gorgonzola on the lettuce. Drizzle with some of the dressing and serve, passing the remaining dressing on the side.

Change it up You can use sliced roast beef in place of the chicken. For delicious on-the-go wraps, arrange the salad ingredients on flour tortillas or sheets of lavash flatbread, dress them lightly with the vinaigrette, and then roll them up.

The cheesesteak—thin slices of griddled beef, a healthy dose of peppers and onions, and cheese heaped on a toasted roll—is a Philadelphia treat that has made its way onto menus all across America. Have plenty of napkins at hand to catch inevitable drips.

CHEESESTEAKS

Makes 4 sandwiches

Boneless beef top loin or rib-eye steak, 1¼ pounds (625 g), in one piece

Olive oil, 2 tablespoons

Yellow onion, 1 large, halved and thinly sliced

Red bell pepper, 1 large, seeded and thinly sliced crosswise

Garlic, 2 cloves, minced

Kosher salt and freshly ground pepper

Canola oil for cooking

Provolone cheese, 6 ounces (185 g), thinly sliced

Crusty French or Italian rolls, 4, split

Freeze the meat until it is firm but not frozen, about 1 hour. Partially freezing the beef makes it easier to slice thinly. Using a sharp, thin-bladed knife, cut the meat across the grain into slices ¼ inch (6 mm) thick. Using a meat pounder, pound the meat until it is a uniform ⅛ inch (3 mm) thick or thinner. Cut into pieces about 4 by 3 inches (10 cm by 7.5 cm).

Meanwhile, in a frying pan, heat the olive oil over medium heat. Add the onion and bell pepper and stir well. Cover, reduce the heat to medium-low, and cook, stirring occasionally, until very tender, 25–30 minutes. Uncover and stir in the garlic. Cook until the garlic is tender, 2–3 minutes more. Season with salt and pepper. Set aside.

Preheat the broiler. Heat a large griddle or 2 frying pans over medium-high heat until hot. Lightly oil the griddle, or add 1 tablespoon oil to each frying pan and tilt to coat the bottoms evenly with the oil. Add the meat slices and cook until browned on the undersides, about 1 minute. Turn the meat slices and divide on the griddle into 4 equal mounds. Top each mound with an equal amount of the Provolone.

Cook until the undersides of the mounds are browned and the cheese is beginning to melt, about 1 minute longer.

Meanwhile, place the rolls, split side up, on a baking sheet and toast in the broiler until lightly crisped, about 1 minute. Transfer the rolls to plates. Using a metal spatula, transfer each mound of beef and cheese onto a toasted roll bottom. Spoon an equal amount of the onion-pepper mixture onto each mound, place the top of the roll on top, and serve at once.

Change it up
Mozzarella, mild Cheddar, and Monterey Jack cheese are all good choices to replace the provolone. Instead of the onion-pepper mixture, cook only one or the other. Or, top the mounds of beef and cheese with warm marinara sauce.

This rustic recipe, combining zesty sauce and tender meatballs inside a crusty roll, all covered with melted cheese, would make any Italian nonna proud. Lighten up this ultra-enticing meal by making the meatballs with ground turkey or chicken.

MEATBALL HOAGIES

Makes 6 sandwiches

Olive oil, 1 tablespoon

Yellow onion, ½ cup (3 oz/90 g) minced

Garlic, 2 cloves, minced

Coarse fresh bread crumbs, ¾ cup (3 oz/90 g)

Whole milk, ½ cup (4 oz/125 ml)

Large egg, 1, beaten

Fresh flat-leaf parsley, 2 tablespoons minced

Dried oregano, 1½ teaspoons

Kosher salt, 1½ teaspoons

Freshly ground pepper, ½ teaspoon

Ground beef round, 1 pound (500 g)

Ground pork and veal, ½ pound (250 g) *each*

Marinara Sauce (page 215 or purchased), 6 cups (48 fl oz/1.5 l)

Crusty Italian rolls, 6, split

Provolone or mozzarella cheese, ½ pound (250 g)

Freshly grated Parmesan cheese, for sprinkling

Preheat the oven to 400°F (200°C). Lightly oil a rimmed baking sheet. In a small frying pan, heat the oil over medium heat. Add the onion and cook, stirring occasionally, until softened, about 4 minutes. Add the garlic and cook until fragrant, about 1 minute more. Transfer to a large bowl and let cool to lukewarm.

Meanwhile, place the bread crumbs in a bowl. Add the milk and let stand for about 5 minutes. Transfer the mixture to a sieve and drain, pressing hard on the bread to extract the excess milk. Add the soaked bread crumbs, egg, parsley, oregano, salt, and pepper to the onion mixture and mix well. Add the ground meats and mix with your hands just until combined. Do not overmix, or the meatballs will be dense.

Using wet hands, shape the mixture into 18 meatballs, and arrange on the prepared baking sheet. Bake until the tops are browned, about 20 minutes, then turn and bake until cooked through, 15 minutes more. Remove from the oven.

In a large saucepan, bring the marinara sauce to a simmer over medium heat. Add the meatballs. Discard any fat on the baking sheet, add ½ cup (4 fl oz/125 ml) boiling water to the baking sheet, and use a wooden spatula to scrape up any browned bits. Pour into the marinara sauce and stir. Simmer until the flavors are blended, about 20 minutes.

Preheat the broiler. Place the rolls, cut sides up, on another rimmed baking sheet. Place 3 meatballs on each roll, then spoon some of the sauce over the meatballs. Pour 2 cups (16 fl oz/500 ml) of the remaining sauce into a bowl and keep warm. Reserve the remaining sauce for another use. Thinly slice the provolone and divide evenly among the sandwiches. Broil until the cheese melts, about 1 minute. Using a large, wide spatula, transfer the hoagies to individual plates. Sprinkle each sandwich with Parmesan cheese and serve, passing the sauce on the side.

Lighten it up Add fresh or frozen thawed spinach to the sauce for an extra serving of vegetables. You can also add a topping of sautéed peppers and onions, such as the mixture used in Cheesesteaks (page 22), after you've melted the cheese.

For many Americans, one bite of an egg salad sandwich, with a filling that dribbles out between the bread slices, is what transports them back to their childhood. Packed with protein and mixed with a healthy dose of fresh herbs, this already healthful sandwich, can be improved with the substitution of whole-wheat bread.

EGG SALAD SANDWICHES

Makes 4 sandwiches

Large eggs, 8

Mayonnaise (page 216 or purchased), ½ cup (4 fl oz/125 ml) plus more for the bread

Celery, 2 small stalks, finely chopped

Green onions, 2 small, white and green parts, finely chopped

Fresh flat-leaf parsley, 1 tablespoon minced

Dijon mustard, 1 teaspoon

Kosher salt and freshly ground pepper

Good-quality white bread, 8 slices

Butter lettuce, 4 leaves

To hard-boil the eggs, place them in a saucepan just large enough to hold them. Add cold water to cover by 1 inch (2.5 cm) and bring just to a boil over high heat. Remove the pan from the heat and cover. Let stand for 15 minutes. Drain the eggs, then transfer to a bowl of ice water and let cool completely.

In a bowl, mix together the ½ cup (4 fl oz/125 ml) mayonnaise, the celery, green onions, parsley, and mustard. Peel the eggs and chop finely. Add to the mayonnaise mixture and mix gently. Season with salt and pepper.

Spread 4 of the bread slices with equal amounts of the egg salad, then top each with a lettuce leaf. Spread mayonnaise on the remaining 4 bread slices, and place, mayonnaise side down, on each sandwich. Cut in half and serve.

Lighten it up Add chopped fresh herbs, such as tarragon, chervil, or chives, to the egg salad. For easy appetizers, spoon the egg salad into Belgian endive leaves, or for a lunchtime salad, mound it onto a bed of lettuce.

This classic can easily be lightened—substitute in low-fat cheese and whole-wheat bread, or skip the bread entirely for thick slices of firm beefsteak tomatoes—without compromising on the gooey delight of a fork-and-knife-required open-face sandwich.

TUNA MELTS

Makes 4 sandwiches

White albacore tuna packed in oil or water, 3 cans (6 ounces/ 185 g each)

Mayonnaise (page 216 or purchased), ½ cup (4 fl oz/125 ml)

Celery, ½ cup (3 oz/90 g) minced

Yellow or red onion, ¼ cup (1.5 oz/45 g) minced

Fresh flat-leaf parsley, 2 tablespoons minced

Freshly ground pepper

Firm white sandwich bread, 4 large slices

Tomato, 8 slices

Mild Cheddar cheese, 6 ounces (185 g), thinly sliced

Preheat the broiler. Drain the tuna well and put in a bowl. Add the mayonnaise, celery, onion, and parsley and stir well. Season with pepper.

Arrange the bread slices on a rimmed baking sheet and broil, turning once, until very lightly browned on both sides, about 1 minute total. Spread equal amounts of the tuna mixture onto each toasted bread slice. Divide the tomato slices evenly among the sandwiches, then divide the Cheddar evenly on top. Return to the broiler and broil until the Cheddar melts, about 1 minute more. Serve at once.

Change it up   You can use rye bread or split English muffins for your tuna melts, and substitute sharp Cheddar, Gruyère, or Swiss cheese for the mild Cheddar. To impart a little tang to the tuna mixture, stir in 2 tablespoons chopped bread-and-butter pickles. If your idea of a tuna melt is not open faced, using untoasted bread, prepare the sandwiches as directed, topping them with a second slice of bread. Spread softened butter on the outside of each sandwich and cook it in a frying pan over medium heat until the cheese melts and the bread is golden brown on both sides.

These rolls are sure to conjure up memories of summers at the shore. Wait until summertime, when lobsters are plentiful and reasonably priced, to make these delicious rolls. You can omit the buns for a bed of crisp, fresh lettuce, so as not to distract from the fabulously flavored lobster.

LOBSTER ROLLS

Makes 4 rolls

Kosher salt

Live lobsters, 2
(1½–2 pounds/
750 g–1 kg each)

**Mayonnaise (page 216 or
purchased),** ¼ cup
(2 fl oz/60 ml)

Fresh lemon juice,
2 teaspoons

Fresh tarragon,
1 teaspoon minced

Fresh flat-leaf parsley,
1 teaspoon minced

Celery salt

Freshly ground pepper

**Hot dog buns, preferably
New England–style
split-top buns,** 4

Unsalted butter,
4 tablespoons (2 oz/60 g),
at room temperature

Fill a very large pot with lightly salted water and bring to a boil over high heat. Add the lobsters and cover. Return to a boil, then remove the lid. Boil until the lobsters are bright red, about 6 minutes. Drain and rinse under cold running water.

Place 1 cooked lobster, back side up, on a cutting board. Slip the tip of a large chef's knife into the lobster at the point where the head meets the body. Holding the lobster securely, cut the head in half lengthwise. Repeat at the other end of the lobster, cutting the body and tail in half lengthwise. Twist the legs and claws from the body. Discard any visceral matter from the body, then remove the meat from the body and tail shells. Using a lobster cracker or nutcracker, crack the claws and any large legs, and remove the meat from the shells. Repeat with the second lobster. Cut the lobster meat into chunks.

In a bowl, combine the lobster meat, mayonnaise, lemon juice, tarragon, and parsley and mix gently. Season with celery salt and pepper. Cover and refrigerate until chilled, at least 2 hours.

Heat a griddle or large, heavy frying pan over medium-high heat. Spread the outside top and bottom of the buns with the butter. Place the buns in the frying pan and cook, turning once, until golden brown on both sides, about 1 minute per side.

Fill each bun with an equal amount of the lobster mixture. Serve at once.

Lighten it up Add 1 celery stalk, minced, to the lobster mixture or top the rolls with 1 cup (1 oz/30 g) shredded iceberg lettuce. To keep it simple, omit the mayonnaise, lemon, and herbs and serve the buns loaded with the lobster meat only and drizzled with plenty of melted butter. Or, change the seafood: use ¾ pound (375 g) fresh-cooked lump crabmeat or cooked, peeled, and deveined shrimp, coarsely chopped, for the lobster meat.

The best fried chicken cutlets are always crisp, juicy, and perfectly seasoned. Here, they are the stars of hearty sandwiches topped with dill pickles and crisp lettuce, a nod to similar ones you might find in luncheonettes throughout the south. Low-fat mayonnaise and whole-wheat buns make this deep-fried favorite a little lighter.

FRIED CHICKEN SANDWICHES

Makes 4 sandwiches

Kosher salt, ½ teaspoon

Freshly ground pepper, ¼ teaspoon

Sweet or hot paprika, preferably Hungarian or Spanish, ¼ teaspoon

Boneless, skinless chicken breast halves, 4 (about 6 ounces/ 185 g each)

Large eggs, 2

Whole milk, ½ cup (4 fl oz/125 ml)

All-purpose flour, 1½ cups (7½ oz/235 g)

Peanut or canola oil, for frying

Soft torpedo or sandwich rolls, 4, split

Mayonnaise (page 216 or purchased), for spreading

Dill pickles, 1 or 2, cut into 12 slices

Red-leaf lettuce, 4 large leaves

Mix together the salt, pepper, and paprika. Using a meat pounder, pound the chicken breasts until they are a uniform ½ inch (12 mm) thick. Cut each breast half in half lengthwise, and sprinkle the pieces evenly with the salt mixture. Let stand at room temperature for 30 minutes, or wrap with plastic wrap and refrigerate overnight.

Have ready a rimmed baking sheet. In a shallow bowl, whisk together the eggs and milk. Put the flour into a second shallow bowl. One at a time, coat the chicken pieces with the flour, shaking off the excess, then dip into the egg mixture, allowing the excess to drip off. Coat with flour a second time, again shaking off the excess. Transfer to the baking sheet.

Preheat the broiler. Pour oil to a depth of ½ inch (12 mm) into a large cast-iron or other heavy frying pan and heat over medium-high heat to 375°F (190°C) on a deep-frying thermometer. Set a large wire rack on another rimmed baking sheet and place near the stove.

In batches if necessary to avoid crowding, carefully slip the chicken pieces into the hot oil and cook, turning once, until golden brown on both sides, about 10 minutes total. Using tongs or a slotted spatula, transfer to the rack to drain.

Meanwhile, place the rolls, split side up, on a baking sheet and toast under the broiler until lightly crisped, about 1 minute. Transfer the toasted rolls to plates. Spread mayonnaise on the cut sides of the rolls. Divide the fried chicken, pickles, and lettuce evenly among the rolls. Serve at once.

Lighten it up   These sandwiches are also delicious topped with slaw instead of pickles and lettuce. Use either Creamy Coleslaw (page 167) or the more vinegary option offered as a "spin" with the Fish Tacos (page 140).

A po'boy, a soft roll stuffed to the brim with the hot filling of your choice, is one of the best sandwiches. Sometimes it's best not to change a classic, and although this Louisiana favorite is great with spicy sausage or sliced roast beef dripping with gravy, it was the original deep-fried oyster filling that put this favorite on the map.

FRIED OYSTER PO'BOYS

Makes 4 sandwiches

Shucked oysters, 1 pound (500 g)

Yellow cornmeal, preferably stone-ground, 1 cup (5 oz/155 g)

All-purpose flour, 1 cup (5 oz/155 g)

Kosher salt, 1¼ teaspoons

Sweet paprika, preferably Hungarian or Spanish, ½ teaspoon

Dried basil, ½ teaspoon

Dried thyme, ½ teaspoon

Freshly ground black pepper, ½ teaspoon

Granulated garlic, ¼ teaspoon

Cayenne pepper, ⅛ teaspoon

Large eggs, 3

Canola oil, for deep-frying

Soft French or Italian rolls, 4, split

Rémoulade (page 213)

Shredded iceberg lettuce, for serving

Tomato slices, for serving

Drain the oysters in a sieve, then rinse well. In a food processor, process the cornmeal until finely ground, about 2 minutes. Pour into a bowl, add the flour, salt, paprika, basil, thyme, black pepper, garlic, and cayenne pepper, and whisk to combine. In another bowl, whisk the eggs until well blended.

Pour oil to a depth of at least 3 inches (7.5 cm) into a large, heavy saucepan and heat over high heat to 350°F (180°C) on a deep-frying thermometer. Preheat the oven to 200°F (95°C).

Meanwhile, line a rimmed baking sheet with parchment paper. A few at a time, dip the oysters into the eggs, then toss in the flour mixture, shaking off the excess. Place on the prepared baking sheet.

Set a large wire rack on another baking sheet and place near the stove. In batches to avoid crowding, carefully slip the oysters into the hot oil and deep-fry, turning once, until golden brown, about 2½ minutes. Using a wire skimmer or slotted spoon, transfer the fried oysters to the rack and keep warm in the oven. Repeat with the remaining oysters.

Remove the oysters from the oven and turn on the broiler. Place the rolls, split side up, on a baking sheet, and toast in the broiler until lightly crisped, 1–2 minutes.

Spread the cut side of each roll half with about 2 tablespoons of the rémoulade. Place an equal number of oysters on the bottom half of each roll, and top with the tomato slices and lettuce. Place the top of the roll on top. Serve at once, passing the remaining rémoulade on the side.

Change it up Not an oyster fan? Substitute 1 pound (500 g) medium shrimp, peeled and deveined, for the oysters. Tartar sauce or a mixture of ketchup and mayonnaise can stand in for the rémoulade.

This well-balanced sandwich, comprised of vegetables, in the form of crunchy lettuce and thick, juicy tomato slices, healthy fats from buttery avocado, bacon protein, and fueling whole-wheat carbohydrates, has proven to be a classic favorite, and is still one of the best ways to spend your lunch break.

BLTA SANDWICHES

Makes 4 sandwiches

Applewood-smoked bacon, 12 thick slices

Whole-wheat or multigrain bread, 8 slices

Mayonnaise (page 216 or purchased), for spreading

Avocados, 2 small

Kosher salt and freshly ground pepper

Beefsteak tomato, 8 slices

Red-leaf lettuce, 4 leaves

Preheat the oven to 400°F (200°C). Arrange the bacon in a single layer on a rimmed baking sheet. Bake until the bacon is crisp and browned, about 20 minutes. Transfer the bacon to paper towels to drain. (Alternatively, fry the bacon on a griddle or in a large frying pan over medium heat until crisp.)

Preheat the broiler. Arrange the bread on a baking sheet. Broil, turning once, until toasted on both sides, about 3 minutes. Transfer the bread to a work surface.

Spread mayonnaise on one side of each bread slice. Halve, pit, and peel the avocados. Place an avocado half, cut side down, on top of 4 of the bread slices. Slice the avocado directly on the bread, taking care not to cut into the bread, then fan out the slices. Season with salt and pepper. Top each avocado half with 3 bacon slices, cut to fit; 2 tomato slices; and 1 lettuce leaf. Place 1 bread slice, mayonnaise side down, atop each lettuce leaf. Cut each sandwich in half and serve.

Lighten it up These same sandwich ingredients can be transformed into a salad by using a little less bread and a little more lettuce. Cut 4 bread slices into cubes, coat with a drizzle of olive oil, and toast under the broiler to make croutons. Toss the sliced avocados and tomatoes, croutons, torn lettuce, and chopped bacon with your favorite vinaigrette (hold the mayo).

The best crab cakes are crispy on the outside, tender on the inside, and bursting with fresh seafood flavor. These plump cakes are loaded with sweet crabmeat, with just enough additional ingredients to flavor and bind them, ensuring that this low-calorie crustacean remains the star.

CRAB CAKES WITH LEMON AIOLI

Makes 4 servings

Mayonnaise (page 216 or purchased), 1 cup (8 fl oz/250 ml)

Finely grated lemon zest, from 1 lemon

Fresh lemon juice, 2 tablespoons

Garlic, 1 clove, minced

Fine sea salt and freshly ground pepper

Fresh-cooked lump crabmeat, 1 pound (500 g)

Panko or other dried bread crumbs, ¾ cup (3 oz/90 g)

Large egg, 1, beaten

Dijon mustard, 1 tablespoon

Worcestershire sauce, 2 teaspoons

Hot pepper sauce, ¼ teaspoon

Fresh flat-leaf parsley, 1 tablespoon chopped

Canola oil, ½ cup (4 fl oz/125 ml)

Lemon wedges, for serving

To make the lemon aioli, in a small bowl, mix together the mayonnaise, lemon zest and juice, and garlic. Season with salt and pepper. Set aside ¼ cup (2 fl oz/60 ml) of the aioli. Cover and refrigerate the remaining aioli until serving.

Line a rimmed baking sheet with parchment paper. To make the crab cakes, pick over the crabmeat for shell shards and cartilage. In a bowl, mix together ¼ cup (1 oz/30 g) of the panko, the reserved ¼ cup (2 fl oz/60 ml) aioli, the egg, mustard, Worcestershire sauce, hot pepper sauce, and parsley. Add the crabmeat and mix gently until combined.

Divide the mixture into 8 equal portions and shape each portion into a thick cake. Spread the remaining ½ cup (2 oz/60 g) panko in a shallow dish. Coat the cakes evenly with the panko, and transfer to the prepared baking sheet. Refrigerate for 15 minutes.

In a large frying pan, heat the oil over medium-high heat until it shimmers. Add the cakes and cook until the undersides are golden brown, 2—3 minutes. Flip the cakes and cook until the other sides are golden brown, about 2 minutes more. Using a slotted spatula, transfer to paper towels to drain briefly.

Serve the crab cakes at once with the lemon wedges and pass the remaining lemon aioli on the side.

Lighten it up   Instead of the aioli, serve the crab cakes with homemade Mayonnaise (page 216) or a simple lemon vinaigrette. Or, make a creamy green goddess dressing: Whisk together 1 cup (8 fl oz/250 ml) mayonnaise; 1 tablespoon *each* minced fresh tarragon, chives, and parsley; 1 teaspoon anchovy paste; 1 teaspoon Dijon mustard; and the grated zest of 1 lemon.

Piled high with such delicatessen staples as corned beef, tangy sauerkraut, and creamy Russian dressing, this sandwich is a comfort food classic. Fermented foods, like sauerkraut, have been known to support the health of your gut, so pile on extra and go light on the Russian dressing to feel better about your sandwich choice.

REUBEN SANDWICHES

Makes 4 sandwiches

Mayonnaise (page 216 or purchased), ⅔ cup (5⅓ oz/170 ml)

Ketchup-style chili sauce or ketchup, ¼ cup (2 oz/60 g)

Bread-and-butter pickles, 2 tablespoons finely chopped

Cooked corned beef (page 101 or purchased), about ¾ pound (375 g), sliced

Rye bread, 8 slices

Swiss cheese, 8 slices

Refrigerated sauerkraut, 1 cup (5 oz/150 g) well drained

Unsalted butter, ½ cup (4 oz/125 g), at room temperature

To make the Russian dressing, in a small bowl, mix together the mayonnaise, chili sauce, and chopped pickles. Set aside.

To make the sandwiches, preheat a griddle or 2 large frying pans over medium heat. Add the corned beef and cook, turning occasionally, just until heated but not browned, about 1 minute. Remove from the heat.

Lay the bread slices on a work surface and spread each slice with 1 tablespoon of the dressing. Trim the slices of Swiss to fit the bread slices, then place 1 cheese slice on each of 4 bread slices. Top each with one-fourth of the corned beef, followed by ¼ cup (1¼ oz/40 g) of the sauerkraut, and then 1 more cheese slice. Top with the remaining bread slices, dressing side down. Spread the outside top and bottom of each sandwich with about 2 tablespoons of the butter.

Place the sandwiches on the griddle and reduce the heat to medium-low. Cook until golden brown on the bottoms, about 4 minutes. The sandwiches should cook fairly slowly to allow the bread to brown without burning while the cheese melts. Flip the sandwiches and brown the second sides, about 4 minutes more. Transfer to a cutting board and cut in half. Serve hot, passing the remaining dressing on the side.

Change it up Use pastrami or smoked ham instead of the corned beef, and pumpernickel in place of the rye. Creamy Coleslaw (page 167) is excellent in place of the sauerkraut and cheese, especially with pastrami.

In signature French fashion, this otherwise humble sandwich is drenched in a decadent, cheesy sauce, then broiled in the oven until bubbling and golden. A fried egg on top is the crowning glory. Balance out the richness with a side of lightly dressed leafy greens, such as frisée.

HAM & GRUYÈRE CROQUE MADAME

Makes 4 servings

Unsalted butter,
4 tablespoons (2 oz/60 g)

All-purpose flour,
2 tablespoons

Whole milk, 1 cup
(8 fl oz/250 ml), warmed

**Shredded Gruyère
cheese,** 1 cup
(4 oz/125 g)

Dijon mustard,
5 teaspoons

**Kosher salt and freshly
ground pepper**

Eggs, 4 large

**Good-quality, firm white
sandwich bread,** 8 slices

**Thinly sliced
Black Forest ham,**
½ lb (250 g)

In a small saucepan, melt 2 tablespoons of the butter over medium-low heat. Whisk in the flour until smooth. Let bubble without browning, whisking frequently, for 1 minute. Gradually whisk in the warm milk, raise the heat to medium, and bring to a gentle boil, whisking frequently. Reduce the heat to medium-low and simmer, whisking frequently, until thickened, about 5 minutes. Remove from the heat. Stir in ¾ cup (3 oz/90 g) of the cheese and 1 teaspoon of the mustard. Season with salt and pepper. Transfer to a bowl, placing a piece of plastic wrap directly onto the surface of the sauce, and let cool.

Preheat the oven to 400°F (200°C). Line a rimmed baking sheet with parchment paper. Arrange the bread slices in a single layer and bake, turning once, until toasted on both sides, about 10 minutes. Remove from the oven and set aside.

In a large frying pan, melt the remaining 2 tablespoons butter over medium heat. Crack the eggs into the pan. Season with salt and pepper, cover, reduce the heat to medium-low, and cook until the whites are set, about 2 minutes for sunny-side-up eggs. Or carefully flip the eggs and cook to the desired doneness.

Preheat the broiler. Spread 4 bread slices with the remaining 4 teaspoons mustard.

Add an equal amount of the sliced ham and 1 tablespoon of the sauce to each slice. Top with the remaining bread slices. Return the sandwiches to the prepared baking sheet. Spread the remaining sauce over the tops of the sandwiches, and sprinkle each with 1 tablespoon of the remaining cheese. Broil until the cheese is melted and golden, about 2 minutes. Transfer to individual plates, top each with a fried egg, and serve at once.

Italian panini have been embraced by cooks all over the world. There is something elementally pleasing about biting into its warm and crusty exterior to reach the cheesy insides. Here's a vegetarian version, and if you don't feel like using pesto, add a few arugula leaves to each one before cooking.

ROASTED VEGETABLE & GOAT CHEESE PANINI

Makes 4 panini

Italian eggplant, 2 small, about 5 ounces (155 g) each, trimmed

Zucchini, 1 large

Red bell pepper, 1 large

Yellow onion, 1, cut into ½-inch (12-mm) half-moons

Extra-virgin olive oil, 2 tablespoons plus more for greasing

Kosher salt and freshly ground pepper

Soft oblong rolls, 4, split lengthwise, excess crumbs removed

Basil Pesto (page 215 or purchased), 4 tablespoons (2¼ oz/60 g)

Goat cheese, 5 ounces (155 g) crumbled

Preheat the oven to 425°F (220°C). Cut each eggplant lengthwise into 3 or 4 strips about ½-inch (12-mm) thick. Repeat with the zucchini. Cut the top and bottom from the bell pepper to make "lids." Make a cut down the side of the pepper and open it up into a long strip. Discard the ribs and seeds.

On an oiled large rimmed baking sheet, place the eggplant and zucchini. Add the bell pepper strip and its lids, skin sides up. Heap sliced onion in a mound on the sheet. Drizzle the onion mound with about 2 teaspoons of the oil, then use the remaining oil to brush the tops of the eggplant and zucchini.

Roast the vegetables for 15 minutes. Gently stir the onions and flip the eggplant and zucchini over and continue roasting until the vegetables are tender, about 20 minutes more. Let cool for 5 minutes. Discard the skin from the pepper pieces. Season the warm vegetables with salt and pepper. Turn the oven temperature to 200°F (95°C).

Spread each roll with 1 tablespoon of pesto. Divide the vegetables, cut as needed to fit the rolls, among the rolls, and sprinkle with the goat cheese. Close the rolls, pressing hard to compact them.

Heat a grill pan or heavy frying pan over medium-high heat, or heat a panini press. Add 2 sandwiches. Place another heavy pan on the sandwiches to weight them down. Cook, adjusting the heat as needed so the panini do not brown too quickly, until the undersides are lightly browned, 2—3 minutes. Flip the sandwiches, weight them with the pan, and brown the other sides until the cheese melts, about 2 minutes more. If using a panini press, the total cooking time will be 4—5 minutes. Remove from the pan and transfer to a baking sheet; keep warm in the oven while cooking the remaining sandwiches in the same way.

A grilled cheese sandwich, with its crunchy exterior and melting center, is high on my list of comfort foods. Since it's comprised of just a few simple ingredients, quality will make all the difference, so seek out a true farmhouse Cheddar, some seriously thick applewood-smoked bacon, and the juiciest tomatoes you can find.

GRILLED CHEDDAR SANDWICHES WITH BACON & TOMATO

Makes 2 sandwiches

Applewood-smoked bacon, 4–6 thick slices

Country-style bread, 4 slices

Sharp farmhouse Cheddar cheese, ¼ lb (125 g), thinly sliced

Ripe tomato, 4 thick slices, drained on paper towels

Unsalted butter, 2 tablespoons, at room temperature

In a large frying pan, fry the bacon over medium heat until crisp and brown, about 8 minutes. Transfer to paper towels to drain. Discard the fat in the pan. Cut each bacon slice in half crosswise.

Lay two of the bread slices on a work surface and top each with one-fourth of the cheese, 2 slices of tomato, half of the bacon, and the remaining cheese. Top with the remaining two bread slices. Spread the outsides of each sandwich with 1 tablespoon of the butter.

Return the frying pan to medium heat. Add the sandwiches. Place a flat lid or a heatproof plate on the sandwiches to weight them down. Cook until the undersides are golden brown and the cheese starts to melt, about 2 minutes. Flip the sandwiches, weight them down with the lid, and brown the other sides, about 2 minutes more. Cut each sandwich in half and serve at once.

Italian-style Panini, which are essentially embellished grilled cheese sandwiches, are endlessly adaptable to any palette. Roasted red peppers and slices of baked eggplant can replace the prosciutto for a delicious vegetarian version. For a Spanish twist, substitute the pesto for romesco sauce and the mozzarella for manchego.

GRILLED PANINI WITH PROSCIUTTO & MOZZARELLA

Makes 4 panini

Firm white country bread, 8 slices

Basil Pesto (page 215 or purchased), 6 tablespoons (3 oz/90 g)

Fresh whole-milk mozzarella, ½ lb (250 g), thinly sliced

Prosciutto, ½ lb (250 g), thinly sliced

Unsalted butter, ¼ cup (2 oz/60 g), at room temperature

Lay the bread slices on a work surface and spread each slice with the pesto, dividing it evenly. Divide the cheese and prosciutto evenly among 4 of the bread slices. Top with the remaining bread slices. Spread each sandwich on both sides with 1 tablespoon of the butter.

Preheat the oven to 200°F (95°C). Heat a grill pan or heavy frying pan over medium-high heat, or heat a panini press. Add 2 sandwiches. Place another heavy pan on the sandwiches to weight them down. Cook, adjusting the heat as needed so the panini do not brown too quickly, until the undersides are lightly browned, 2–3 minutes. Flip the sandwiches, weight them with the pan, and brown the other sides until the cheese melts, about 2 minutes more. If using a panini press, the total cooking time will be 4–5 minutes. Remove from the pan and transfer to a baking sheet; keep warm in the oven while cooking the remaining sandwiches in the same way.

Cut each sandwich in half diagonally and serve at once.

Change it up If you aren't in the mood for prosciutto, other Italian-style cured meats, such as salami and mortadella, also make wonderful panini.

Here, creamy hazelnut-chocolate spread replaces jam in this revamped, dessert-worthy version of the classic PB&J. Griddling the sandwich transform 4 simple ingredients into an irresistible dish, perfect for quartering and serving as snacks with milk, or enjoying as a decadent midday treat.

GRILLED PB & CHOCOLATE SANDWICHES

Makes 4 sandwiches

Good-quality white bread, 8 slices

Creamy or crunchy peanut butter, about ½ cup (5 oz/155 g)

Chocolate-hazelnut spread, such as Nutella®, about ½ cup (5 oz/155 g)

Unsalted butter, 4 tablespoons (2 oz/60 g), at room temperature

Place the bread slices on a work surface. Spread 4 of the slices with the peanut butter. Spread the other 4 slices with the chocolate-hazelnut spread, and place each slice, chocolate side down, on a peanut butter slice. Heat a griddle or 2 frying pans over medium heat until hot. Spread the outside of each sandwich with 1 tablespoon of the butter. Place on the griddle, reduce the heat to medium-low, and cook until the undersides are golden brown, about 3 minutes. Flip the sandwiches and brown the other side, 3 minutes more. Cut in half and serve.

Change it up Add a thin layer of jam—raspberry or apricot are delicious—or a layer of sliced banana. Spread the jam or the banana slices on the peanut butter before topping with the chocolate-hazelnut spread.

Filled with a mixture of creamy ricotta and sautéed spinach and onions, these calzone are fun to eat out of hand. Or, if you like, outfit diners with knives and forks and serve them with a side of tangy marinara sauce (page 215) for dipping, just like you might find at a classic Italian American pizzeria.

RICOTTA & SPINACH CALZONE

Makes 4-6 servings

Pizza Dough (page 216)

Baby spinach, 10 ounces (315 g)

Olive oil, 2 tablespoons plus more for brushing

Yellow onion, 1, minced

Garlic, 2 cloves, minced

Parmesan cheese, ½ cup (2 oz/60 g) freshly grated

Fresh mozzarella cheese, ¼ pound (125 g), finely diced

Ricotta cheese, 1 cup (8 oz/250 g)

Kosher salt and freshly ground pepper

All-purpose or bread flour for dusting

The night before serving, prepare the pizza dough and refrigerate. Remove the dough from the refrigerator 1–2 hours before forming the calzone. To make the filling, rinse the spinach but do not dry it. In a large frying pan, heat the 2 tablespoons oil over medium heat. Add the onion and cook, stirring occasionally, until translucent, about 4 minutes. Stir in the garlic and cook until fragrant, about 1 minute. Add the spinach, cover, and cook until tender, about 3 minutes. Drain the spinach mixture in a sieve, pressing gently to remove excess liquid. Transfer to a bowl, add the Parmesan, mozzarella, and ricotta cheeses, and mix well. Season with salt and pepper.

Position racks in the center and lower third of the oven and preheat to 400°F (200°C). Oil 2 rimmed baking sheets. Divide the pizza dough into 6 equal portions, and shape each portion into a ball. Place the balls on a work surface and cover with a kitchen towel. Place 1 ball on a floured work surface, and roll out into a round 7 inches (18 cm) in diameter. Brush the edges of the round lightly with water. Place one-sixth of the cheese mixture on half of the round, leaving a 1-inch (2.5-cm) border uncovered. Fold the dough over so the edges meet, then crimp with a fork. Pierce the top of the calzone with the fork and transfer to a baking sheet. Repeat with the remaining dough and filling, putting 3 calzone on each baking sheet. Brush the calzone with olive oil.

Bake until golden brown, about 20 minutes. Transfer to wire racks and let cool for 10 minutes. Serve warm.

Change it up   You can fill a calzone with just about any combination of meats, cheeses, and vegetables that you'd put on a pizza. For example, replace the spinach in this recipe with 1 cup (4 oz/120 g) sautéed sliced mushrooms or zucchini, or cooked and crumbled Italian sausage.

Here, we've upgraded a classic childhood pairing from canned soup to a fresh and nutritious homemade variety, infused with flavor-rich roasted plum tomatoes. Keep portions healthy by quartering the sandwiches and serving them atop steaming bowls of soup, as grilled cheese croutons.

GRILLED CHEESE WITH CREAMY TOMATO SOUP

Makes 4 servings

CREAMY TOMATO SOUP

Olive oil, 2 tablespoons

Plum tomatoes, 4 pounds (2 kg)

Celery, 2 stalks

Shallots, 1/3 cup (2 oz/60 g)

Unsalted butter, 1 tablespoon

Chicken Stock (page 212) or broth, 1/2 cup (4 fl oz/125 ml), or as needed

Fresh thyme, 1 teaspoon

Sugar, 1/2 teaspoon

Heavy cream, 1/2 cup (4 fl oz/125 ml)

Kosher salt and freshly ground pepper

GRILLED CHEESE

Mild Cheddar cheese, 3/4 pound (375 g), thinly sliced

Sourdough bread or pain au levain, 8 slices

Unsalted butter, 4 tablespoons (2 oz/60 g), at room temperature

To make the soup, preheat the oven to 400°F (200°C). Lightly oil a rimmed baking sheet. Cut the tomatoes in half lengthwise. Finely chop the celery and shallots. Place them, cut side up, on the prepared baking sheet and brush with the 2 tablespoons oil. Roast until the tomatoes look somewhat shriveled, about 45 minutes. Let cool for about 20 minutes. Transfer the tomatoes and any juices to a food processor. Pulse until chopped, then rub the tomatoes and their juices through a coarse-mesh sieve placed over a bowl. You should have about 3 1/2 cups (20 oz/625 g) tomato purée. Discard the contents of the sieve.

In a large saucepan, melt the butter over medium-low heat. Add the celery and cook, stirring occasionally, until tender, about 5 minutes. Add the shallots and cook, stirring occasionally, until softened, about 3 minutes. Stir in the tomato purée, stock, and thyme and bring to a simmer over medium-high heat. Reduce the heat to medium-low and simmer, uncovered, for about 15 minutes. Stir in the sugar. In 3 or 4 batches, transfer the soup to a blender and process until smooth. Transfer to a clean saucepan, add the cream, and heat until piping hot but not boiling. If the soup seems thick, thin with more stock. Season to taste with salt and pepper.

To make the grilled cheese sandwiches, heat a griddle or 2 large frying pans over medium heat until hot. For each sandwich, place one-fourth of the cheese on top of 1 bread slice and top with a second bread slice. Spread the outsides of each sandwich with 1 tablespoon of the butter. Place on the griddle, reduce the heat to medium-low, and cook until the undersides are golden brown, 3—4 minutes. Flip the sandwiches and brown the other side, 3—4 minutes more. Ladle the soup into warmed bowls. Serve at once, with the hot sandwiches alongside.

Change it up Grilled cheese sandwiches offer countless variations: use your favorite bread or different cheeses. For an over-the-top sandwich, add ham and tomato slices before grilling. Drizzle flavored olive oil on top of single servings of soup, if you wish.

Meltingly tender onions, meaty stock, and rich, nutty melted cheese—these are the indispensable elements that make this boldly flavored soup a hallmark of French cuisine—and a favorite of American tables, too. Take the time to make your own stock and you will be rewarded with deep flavor and savory goodness.

FRENCH ONION SOUP

Makes 8 servings

Unsalted butter, 2 tablespoons

Yellow onions, 2½ pounds (1.25 kg), halved and thinly sliced

All-purpose flour, 1 tablespoon

Dry white wine, 1 cup (8 fl oz/250 ml)

Beef Stock (page 212) or broth, 8 cups (64 fl oz/2 l)

Fresh thyme, 2 teaspoons minced, or 1 teaspoon dried

Bay leaf, 1

Kosher salt and freshly ground pepper

Crusty baguette, 1

Gruyère cheese, 2⅔ cups (10½ oz/335 g) shredded

In a large, heavy sauté pan, melt the butter over medium heat. Add the onions, stir well, cover, and cook for 5 minutes. Uncover, reduce the heat to medium-low, and cook, stirring occasionally, until tender and deep golden brown, about 30 minutes.

Sprinkle the flour over the onions and stir until combined. Gradually stir in the wine, then the stock, and finally the thyme and bay leaf. Bring to a boil over high heat, reduce the heat to medium-low, and simmer, uncovered, until slightly reduced, about 30 minutes. Season with salt and pepper. Discard the bay leaf.

Meanwhile, preheat the broiler. Have ready eight 1½-cup (12-fl oz/375-ml) broilerproof soup crocks. Cut the baguette into 16 slices, sizing them so that 2 slices will fit inside each crock. Arrange the bread slices on a baking sheet and broil, turning once, until lightly toasted on both sides, about 1 minute total. Set the slices aside. Position the oven rack about 12 inches (30 cm) from the heat source, and leave the broiler on.

Ladle the hot soup into the crocks. Place 2 toasted bread slices, overlapping if necessary, on top of the soup and sprinkle each crock evenly with about ⅓ cup (1⅓ oz/40 g) of the Gruyère. Broil until the cheese is bubbling, about 2 minutes. Serve at once.

Change it up For an extra layer of flavor and complexity, instead of the yellow onions, use a mixture of roughly equal amounts red, white, and sweet (such as Vidalia) onions. Italy's Fontina cheese, from the Val d'Aosta, is a delicious alternative to the traditional Gruyère cheese.

Dipping in to a steaming bowl of cream of vegetable soup is the culinary equivalent of wrapping yourself in a warm blanket. A purée of vegetables with a finish of melted Cheddar gives this soup its smoothness. The cornstarch coating for the cheese helps it to melt smoothly, so don't leave it out.

BROCCOLI & CHEDDAR SOUP

Makes 8 servings

Vegetable oil, 2 tablespoons

Unsalted butter, 2 tablespoons

Leek, 1, white and pale green part only, chopped

Carrot, 1, chopped

Celery rib, 1, chopped

Garlic, 1 clove, crushed under a knife and peeled

Broccoli, 1 head (about 1¼ pounds/625 g), stems peeled and chopped, tops cut into florets

All-purpose flour, ¼ cup (1½ oz/45 g)

Chicken Stock (page 212) or broth, 6 cups (48 fl oz/1.5 l)

Sharp Cheddar cheese, 2 cups (8 ounces/250 g) shredded

Cornstarch, 4 teaspoons

Kosher salt and freshly ground pepper

In a soup pot, heat the oil and butter together over medium heat until the butter is melted. Add the leek, carrot, celery, and garlic and cover. Cook, stirring occasionally, until the leek is tender, about 5 minutes. Stir in the broccoli.

Sprinkle the broccoli mixture with the flour and mix well. Stir in the broth and bring to a simmer over high heat. Reduce the heat to medium-low and simmer, with the lid ajar, until the broccoli is very tender, about 20 minutes. Remove from the heat.

Using a hand-held blender, process the soup until smooth. (Or, in four or five batches, purée the soup in a blender with the lid ajar and transfer to a large bowl. Be sure to purée the soup in batches with the lid ajar, or the steam could force the lid off the blender. Return the puréed soup to the pot.)

Return the soup to a simmer over medium-low heat. In a medium bowl, toss the Cheddar and cornstarch together to coat the Cheddar. A handful at a time, add the coated Cheddar to the soup, and let it melt. Bring to soup just to a simmer. Season with salt and pepper. Serve hot.

Change it up Cauliflower and Romanesco can be substituted for the broccoli. Try Gruyère instead of the Cheddar cheese. Garnish the soup with mini broccoli florets, if you wish.

Pancetta, garlic, vegetables, and herbs give this soup fragra_____ _r, while the beans and pasta make it hearty. If you can't find fresh bea__ _ (7oz/220 g) dried beans. Rinse the beans, then soak them under 1 inch __ water for at least 4 hours, drain, and increase the cooking time to 45—60 m.

ITALIAN BEAN & PASTA SOUP

Makes 6 servings

Pancetta, ¼ pound (125 g), chopped

Extra-virgin olive oil, 1 tablespoon

Yellow onion, 1, finely chopped

Carrots, 2, diced

Celery, 1 stalk, diced

Garlic, 2 cloves, minced

Chicken Stock (page 212) or broth, 8 cups (64 fl oz/2 l)

Fresh cranberry beans, 1 pound (500 g), shelled

Fresh rosemary sprig, 1

Bay leaf, 1

Parmesan cheese rind, 2-inch (5 cm) piece

Small pasta shapes such as conchigliette or ditalini, ⅔ cup (2⅓ oz/70 g)

Tomatoes, 2, seeded and chopped

Kosher salt and freshly ground pepper

Freshly grated Parmesan cheese, for serving

In a soup pot, cook the pancetta with the oil over medium heat, stirring occasionally, until the pancetta begins to brown, about 5 minutes. Add the onion, carrots, and celery and cook, stirring occasionally, until the vegetables have softened, about 8 minutes. Stir in the garlic and cook until fragrant, about 1 minute.

Pour in the stock and add the beans, rosemary, bay leaf, and Parmesan rind. Raise the heat to medium-high and bring to a boil. Reduce the heat to medium-low, cover, and simmer, stirring occasionally, until the beans are just tender, about 30 minutes.

Stir the pasta and tomatoes into the pot and simmer, stirring occasionally, until the pasta is al dente (check the package directions for cooking time). Discard the rosemary, bay leaf, and Parmesan rind.

Season the soup with salt and pepper, ladle into warmed bowls, and serve at once, passing the Parmesan cheese on the side.

Lighten it up Beef stock (page 212) can be used in place of the chicken stock. Add a spoonful of basil pesto (page 215) to each bowl for a colorful garnish. For a more colorful serving, substitute the pasta for 1 zucchini, diced, and double the amount of carrots and celery.

Chock-full of briny clams and tender chunks of potato, this creamy New England chowder seems custom-made to take the chill off of a cold afternoon. Serve alongside a large green salad to balance out the richness of the soup.

CLAM CHOWDER

Makes 6-8 servings

Littleneck clams, 4 dozen (about 4 pounds/2 kg)

Kosher salt and freshly ground pepper

Red-skinned potatoes, 2 large

Applewood-smoked bacon, 4 thick slices, chopped

Yellow onion, 1 chopped

Celery, 2 small stalks, finely chopped

All-purpose flour, 3 tablespoons

Half-and-half, 2 cups (16 fl oz/500 ml)

Fresh thyme, ½ teaspoon minced

Chopped fresh flat-leaf parsley, for garnish

Scrub the clams under cold running water. Place in a large bowl, add salted cold water to cover, and let stand for 1 hour (this removes any sand or grit, which could spoil the soup). Drain the clams and rinse well. Place the clams in a saucepan and add 1 cup (8 fl oz/250 ml) water. Cover and bring to a boil over high heat. Cook, shaking the pan occasionally, until the clams have opened, about 4 minutes.

Discard any unopened clams. Transfer the clams to a large bowl, reserving the cooking liquid in the pan. Remove the clam meat from the shells, setting the meat aside and discarding the shells. Line a fine-mesh sieve with dampened cheesecloth, place it over a 4-cup (32-fl oz/1-l) glass measuring cup, and strain the cooking liquid from the pan and the large bowl through the cheesecloth. Add cold water as needed to the measuring cup to total 4 cups (32 fl oz/1 l) liquid.

Meanwhile, dice the unpeeled potatoes and place in a large saucepan. Add salted water to cover by 1 inch (2.5 cm), cover the pan, and bring to a boil over high heat. Uncover, reduce the heat to medium-low, and simmer until tender when pierced with a knife, about 20 minutes. Drain and set aside.

In a large saucepan, fry the bacon over medium-low heat, stirring occasionally, until browned, about 10 minutes. Using a slotted spoon, transfer to paper towels to drain. Add the onion and celery to the fat in the pan and cook over medium heat, stirring occasionally, until tender, about 5 minutes. Sprinkle in the flour and stir well. Stir in the reserved potatoes and clam liquid, the half-and-half, and the thyme. Bring to a simmer, reduce the heat to medium-low, and simmer until lightly thickened, about 5 minutes. Stir in the reserved clam meat and bacon, and season with salt and pepper. Ladle into warmed bowls, sprinkle with parsley, and serve.

Change it up To make fish chowder, omit the clams. Replace the clam liquid and water with 4 cups (32 fl oz/1 l) fish stock. Add 1 pound (500 g) skinned fish fillets, such as cod or haddock, cut into 1-inch (2.5-cm) pieces, to the soup along with the cooked potatoes. Simmer until barely opaque, about 5 minutes. Continue the recipe as directed.

Chicken soup is famous with moms around the world for its restorative properties, but this version, with its silky egg noodles and chunks of fresh vegetables, will make you feel good even if you don't have the sniffles.

CHICKEN NOODLE SOUP

Makes 8 servings

Olive oil, 2 tablespoons

Yellow onion, 1, diced

Carrots, 2, diced

Celery, 1 stalk, diced

Chicken Stock (page 212) or broth, 8 cups (64 fl oz/2 l)

Cooked, shredded chicken (from Chicken Stock, page 212 or purchased rotisserie chicken), 4 cups (24 oz/740 g)

Fine sea salt and freshly ground pepper

Egg noodles, 2 cups (12 oz/360 g), cooked and drained

In a soup pot, heat the oil over medium heat. Add the onion, carrots, and celery, cover, and cook, stirring occasionally, until the vegetables soften, about 5 minutes. Add the stock and bring to a boil over high heat. Reduce the heat to medium-low and simmer until the vegetables are tender, about 20 minutes. Add the chicken. Season with salt and pepper.

Stir in the cooked egg noodles. Spoon the soup into warmed large bowls and serve at once.

Change it up Replace the egg noodles with small pasta shapes, such as ditalini, along with the chicken, and heat through. For chicken and rice soup, add cooked long-grain rice and heat through. Don't add uncooked noodles or rice, as they will soak up too much liquid, making the soup too thick.

Flavored boldly with shallots, rosemary, and sage, there's nothing boring about this chicken hash. This healthy hash, in which lean chicken has replaced red meat, is perfect for lunch or brunch, with poached eggs served on top.

CLASSIC CHICKEN HASH

Makes 4-6 servings

Bone-in skin-on chicken breasts, 1¾ lb (875 g)

Chicken Stock (page 212) or broth, 2 cups (16 fl oz/500 ml)

Yellow onion, 1 small, sliced

Kosher salt and freshly ground pepper

Russet potatoes, 1½ lb (750 g), scrubbed

Unsalted butter, 7 tablespoons (3½ oz/105 g)

Red bell pepper, 1, seeded and chopped

Minced shallots, 3 tablespoons

All-purpose flour, 3 tablespoons

Heavy cream, 2 tablespoons

Fresh rosemary and sage, 2 teaspoons *each*, minced

Chopped fresh chives, for garnish

In a large saucepan, combine the chicken, stock, onion, ½ teaspoon salt, and ¼ teaspoon pepper. Add enough cold water to barely cover the chicken. Bring to a boil over high heat. Reduce the heat to medium-low and simmer until the chicken shows no sign of pink when pierced with a sharp knife, about 30 minutes. Transfer to a carving board and let stand until cool enough to handle. Strain the stock through a wire sieve and set aside 1½ cups (12 fl oz/375 ml). Save the remaining stock for another use. Remove and discard the skin and bones from the chicken. Cube the meat and transfer to a large bowl.

Meanwhile, put the potatoes in another saucepan and add enough salted water to cover. Bring to a boil over high heat. Reduce the heat to medium-low, cover, and simmer until the potatoes are tender when pierced with a sharp knife, about 25 minutes. Drain and rinse under cold running water. Let the potatoes cool, then peel and cube. Add to the chicken.

In a large frying pan, melt 2 tablespoons of the butter over medium heat. Add the bell pepper and cook, stirring frequently, until tender, about 5 minutes. Add the shallots and cook until tender, about 2 minutes more. Add to the chicken and potatoes.

In a saucepan, melt 3 tablespoons of the butter over medium-low heat. Whisk in the flour and let bubble for 1 minute without browning. Gradually whisk in the 1½ cups (12 fl oz/375 ml) reserved stock, raise the heat to medium, and bring to a boil, whisking frequently. Reduce the heat to medium-low and cook, whisking frequently, until reduced by about one-third, 8—10 minutes. Stir in the cream. Add to the chicken mixture, along with the rosemary and sage, and stir well, breaking up the potatoes with the side of the spoon. Season with salt and pepper.

Add the remaining 2 tablespoons of butter to the frying pan and melt over medium-high heat. Add the chicken mixture, and press it into a flat disk with a metal spatula. Cook until browned and crusty, 4—5 minutes. Using the spatula, turn sections of the hash over (it should not remain whole), and press down. Cook until the second side is browned, 4—5 minutes more. Serve at once, sprinkling each serving with chives.

Thick and warming, split pea soup with little chunks of ham seems to have been created to warm your insides on the coldest day. Simmering ham hocks to make a broth gives the soup great flavor, but because there isn't much meat on the bones, the soup is also bolstered with diced smoked ham.

SPLIT PEA & HAM HOCK SOUP

Makes 8 servings

Canola oil, 1 tablespoon

Yellow onion, 2, chopped

Celery stalk, 2, diced

Carrot, 2, diced

Smoked ham hocks, 1½ pounds (750 g), each sawed by the butcher crosswise into 2 or 3 pieces

Fresh thyme, 2 sprigs or ½ teaspoon dried thyme

Black peppercorns, ¼ teaspoon

Bay leaf, 1

Dried split green peas, 1 pound (500 g)

Unsalted butter, 2 tablespoons

Kosher salt and freshly ground black pepper

Smoked ham, 8 ounces (250 g), cut into bite-sized pieces

To make the ham hock stock, in a soup pot, heat the oil over medium heat. Add half the onions, half the celery, and half the carrots and cook, stirring occasionally, until the vegetables are softened, about 3 minutes. Add the ham hocks, thyme, peppercorns, and bay leaf, and pour in 2 quarts (2 l) cold water. Raise the heat to high and bring to a boil, skimming off any foam that rises to the surface. Reduce the heat to medium-low and simmer until the meat is tender and beginning to fall from the bones, about 1½ hours.

Strain the stock through a colander into a large bowl. Set aside the ham hocks to cool and discard the other solids in the colander. Measure the stock—you should have 7 cups (56 fl oz/1.75 l), so add water if needed. Rinse out the soup pot.

Rinse and drain the peas. Pick them over, discarding any misshapen beans or stones.

Melt the butter in the soup pot over medium heat. Add the remaining half of the onions, celery, and carrots and cook, stirring occasionally, until the vegetables are softened, about 3 minutes. Add the split peas and stock. Add more water, if needed, to cover the ingredients by 1 inch (2.5 cm). Raise the heat to high and bring to a boil. Reduce the heat to medium-low and simmer, stirring occasionally, until the split peas are almost tender, about 40 minutes. Season the soup with salt and pepper.

Remove the meat from the ham hocks and discard the bones. Dice the meat into ½-inch (12-mm) pieces. Add to the soup with the smoked ham. Continue cooking until the peas are very tender and the soup is thick, about 10 minutes more. Serve at once.

Lighten it up Stir 2 tablespoons finely chopped fresh dill into the soup, if you wish. Many cooks prefer smoked turkey wings (have the butcher chop them into 2- to 3-inch (5- to 7.5-cm chunks) to smoked ham hocks, and you can substitute smoked turkey for the ham, too.

This chili, with juicy chunks of tender chicken and plenty of white beans, is every bit as satisfying as the beef version. In fact, many people may actually prefer this lighter variation because of its reduced spiciness. If you wish, offer minced fresh jalapeños on the side for those who might want to ratchet up the heat.

WHITE CHICKEN & CANNELLINI CHILI

Makes 8 servings

Extra-virgin olive oil, 4 tablespoons (2 fl oz/ 60 ml), or more as needed

Yellow onion, 1 large, chopped

Red bell pepper, 1 large, chopped

Jalapeño, 1, seeded and minced

Garlic, 2 cloves, minced

Ground cumin, 1 teaspoon

Chicken thighs, 3 pounds (1.5 kg) skinless, boneless, cut into 1-inch (2.5-cm) chunks

Kosher salt and freshly ground pepper

Chicken Stock (page 212) or broth, 2 cups (16 fl oz/500 ml),

Cannellini beans, 3 cans (15 ounces/470 g each), drained and rinsed

Chopped fresh cilantro, for serving

In a flameproof casserole or Dutch oven, heat 2 tablespoons of the oil over medium high. Add the onion, bell pepper, jalapeño, and garlic and cook, stirring occasionally, until the vegetables are tender, about 5 minutes. Stir in the cumin and cook until fragrant, about 1 minute. Transfer to a bowl.

Add the remaining 2 tablespoons oil to the casserole and heat over medium-high heat. Sprinkle the chicken with 2 teaspoons salt and 1 teaspoon pepper. In batches to avoid crowding, add the chicken and cook, stirring occasionally, adding more oil as needed, until the chicken is browned, about 5 minutes. Using a slotted spoon, transfer the chicken to a bowl with the vegetables.

Pour the stock into the casserole and bring to a boil, scraping up the browned bits on the bottom with a wooden spoon. Return the chicken and vegetables to the casserole and reduce the heat to medium-low. Cover the casserole and simmer until the chicken is almost tender, about 30 minutes. Stir in the beans and cook, stirring occasionally, until the beans are hot and the chicken is tender, about 15 minutes more. Using a large spoon, crush some of the beans to lightly thicken the cooking liquid. Serve in bowls, sprinkling each serving with the cilantro.

Change it up If you wish, substitute 1½ pounds (750 g) sweet or hot Italian turkey or chicken sausage, with the casings removed, for an equal amount of the chicken thighs. Reduce the salt to 1 teaspoon, and only season the thighs as the sausage already contains salt. Cook the sausage, breaking it up with the side of a spoon into bite-sized pieces, until it is lightly browned and loses its raw look, 5 to 7 minutes. Additionally, this chili can be served with crushed dried chilies on the side for those who prefer it.

Chili has a magical ability to warm you up from the inside out. This version is rib-sticking, but doesn't contain an ounce of meat, with a perfect combination of vegetables and legumes. This makes a large batch, all the better to store in the freezer for a quick lunch, supper, or loaded nachos (using the instructions below).

VEGETABLE, CORN & BLACK BEAN CHILI

Makes 6-8 servings

Yellow onion, 1 large

Red bell pepper, 1 large

Zucchini, 2

Celery ribs with leaves, 2

Carrot, 1

Jalapeño, 1, seeded

Canned tomatoes, 1 can (28 ounces/875 g)

Black beans, 2 cans (15½ ounces/485 g)

Extra-virgin olive oil, 2 tablespoons

Garlic, 2 cloves, minced

Chili powder, 2 tablespoons

Ground cumin and dried oregano, 1 teaspoon *each*

Fresh or thawed frozen corn kernels, 1½ cups (9 oz/270 g)

Fresh cilantro, ¼ cup (⅓ oz/10 g) chopped (optional)

Kosher salt and freshly ground pepper

Monterey jack cheese and scallions, for serving

Prep your ingredients for cooking. Chop the yellow onion. Seed the bell pepper. Cut the bell pepper, zucchini, celery, and carrot into ½-inch (12-mm) dice. Finely chop the jalapeño. Chop the canned tomatoes and reserve the juices. Drain and rinse the black beans.

Heat the oil in a large saucepan over medium heat. Add the onion, bell pepper, zucchini, celery, carrot, jalapeño, and garlic and cover. Cook, stirring occasionally, until the vegetables are softened, about 10 minutes. Add the chili powder, cumin, and oregano and stir well. Stir in the tomatoes with their juices and bring to a simmer.

Reduce the heat to low and simmer until the tomato juices are lightly thickened, about 20 minutes. Stir in the beans and corn and cook until they are heated through, about 10 minutes more. Stir in the cilantro, if using. Season with salt and pepper.

Spoon into bowls and serve at once, with bowls of Monterey jack and scallions for passing at the table.

Change it up To make vegetarian chili nachos (shown at right), preheat the broiler. Arrange a layer of tortilla chips on a baking sheet. Scatter a generous serving of the chili and shredded Monterey Jack cheese over the chips. Scatter another layer of chips on top and top with more chili and shredded cheese. Place under the broiler and cook until the cheese is melted, keeping a close eye on the nachos, as they burn easily, 3–7 minutes. Remove from the oven, let cool slightly, then top with sliced jalapeños, fresh cilantro, sour cream, hot sauce, and mashed avocado.

The ever-popular breakfast burrito varies from cook to cook: I like to stuff mine with eggs, black beans, avocado, sour cream, salsa, and always some spicy chorizo sausage. Filled with protein and healthy fats, you probably won't need to eat again until dinnertime. For a lighter version, replace the chorizo with wilted spinach.

BLACK BEAN & CHORIZO BURRITOS

Makes 4 burritos

Fresh Mexican-style chorizo sausage, ¾ lb (375 g), casings removed

Yellow onion, ½ cup (2 oz/60 g) chopped

Red bell pepper, ½ cup (2½ oz/75 g) chopped

Garlic, 1 clove, minced

Black beans, 1 can (15½ oz/485 g), drained and rinsed

Kosher salt and freshly ground pepper

Eggs, 8 large

Unsalted butter, 2 tablespoons

Flour tortillas, 4, each about 9 inches (23 cm) in diameter, warmed

Avocado, 1 ripe, pitted, peeled, and cut into 8 wedges

Sour cream, ½ cup (4 oz/125 g), as needed

Pico de Gallo (page 213), ½ cup (4 oz/125 ml)

In a medium frying pan, cook the chorizo over medium-high heat, breaking it up with the side of a wooden spoon, until it begins to brown, about 8 minutes. Using a slotted spoon, transfer the chorizo to paper towels to drain. Pour off all but 1 tablespoon of the fat from the pan.

Add the onion and bell pepper and cook, stirring occasionally, until tender, about 5 minutes. Stir in the garlic and cook until fragrant, about 1 minute. Return the chorizo to the pan. Add the black beans and stir well. Stir in ½ cup (4 fl oz/125 ml) water. Simmer until the beans are heated through and the liquid is almost completely evaporated, about 5 minutes. Season with salt. Remove from the heat and keep warm.

In a large bowl, whisk together the eggs, ½ teaspoon salt, and ¼ teaspoon pepper. In a large frying pan, preferably nonstick, melt the butter over medium heat. Pour in the eggs and cook until the eggs begin to set, about 20 seconds. Stir with a heatproof spatula, scraping up the eggs on the bottom and sides of the pan and folding them toward the center. Repeat until the eggs are barely cooked into moist curds. Remove the pan from the heat and let the eggs stand in the pan to allow the residual heat to finish cooking them.

Place a warm tortilla on a work surface. Spoon one-fourth of the eggs on the bottom half, leaving a 1-inch (2.5-cm) border. Top with one-fourth of the beans, 2 avocado wedges, about 2 tablespoons of the sour cream, and 2 tablespoons of the pico de gallo. Fold in both sides of the tortilla about 1 inch (2.5 cm). Starting at the bottom, roll up the tortilla to enclose the filling. Repeat with the remaining ingredients. Serve at once.

The first frittata I ever ate had these same toppings, and I fell in love with the Mediterranean flavors of Italian sausage, red bell pepper, and feta cheese, which is why I've been making my frittatas the same way ever since. This one-pot dish makes a beautiful meal served in wedges alongside a green salad.

ROASTED RED PEPPER FRITTATA WITH SAUSAGE & FETA

Makes 4 servings

Olive oil, 2 teaspoons

Sweet Italian sausage, 6 oz (185 g), casing removed

Eggs, 8 large

Fresh basil, 4 teaspoons chopped

Kosher salt and freshly ground pepper

Unsalted butter, 1 tablespoon

Roasted red bell pepper, 1, peeled, seeded, and cut into thin strips

Crumbled feta cheese, ⅓ cup (1½ oz/45 g)

In an ovenproof frying pan, heat the oil over medium heat. Add the sausage and cook, stirring and breaking it up with the side of a wooden spoon, until it begins to brown, about 10 minutes. Using a slotted spoon, transfer the sausage to paper towels to drain. Discard the fat in the pan.

Preheat the broiler. In a bowl, whisk together the eggs, 2 teaspoons of the basil, ½ teaspoon salt, and ¼ teaspoon pepper. Add the butter to the pan and melt over medium heat until hot. Return the sausage to the pan and add the roasted bell pepper. Pour the egg mixture into the sausage mixture and cook over medium heat until the edges of the frittata begin to set, about 30 seconds. Using a heatproof spatula, lift the cooked edges of the frittata, and tilt the frying pan to allow the liquid egg on top to flow underneath. Continue cooking, occasionally lifting the frittata and tilting it again, until the top is almost set, about 4 minutes more.

Sprinkle the top of the frittata with the cheese. Place under the broiler until the frittata puffs and becomes golden brown, about 1 minute. Sprinkle with the remaining basil. Cut into wedges and serve hot or warm.

Perhaps the ultimate brunch dish, this baked egg dish is endlessly versatile. Broccoli and Cheddar are a universally appealing combination, but don't be afraid to experiment with different vegetables, cheeses, and proteins. For a gluten-free option, omit the pastry dough and bake the filling directly in a greased pie dish.

BROCCOLI-CHEDDAR QUICHE

Makes 6 servings

Buttery Pastry Dough (page 217)

Flour, for dusting

Broccoli florets, 2 cups (4 oz/125 g)

Half-and-half, 1 cup (8 fl oz/250 ml)

Eggs, 2 large

Minced fresh dill, 1 tablespoon

Kosher salt and freshly ground pepper

Sharp Cheddar cheese, 1 cup (4 oz/125 g) shredded

Place the dough on a lightly floured work surface and dust the top with flour. (If the dough is chilled hard, let it stand at room temperature for a few minutes until it begins to soften before rolling it out.) Roll out into a round about 12 inches (30 cm) in diameter and about ⅛ inch (3 mm) thick. Transfer to a 9-inch (23-cm) tart pan with a removable bottom, gently fitting the dough into the bottom and sides of the pan. Using scissors or a small knife, trim the dough, leaving a ½-inch (12-mm) overhang. Fold the overhanging dough over and into the pan, pressing it firmly against the sides of the pan; the dough should be doubly thick at the sides and rise about ⅛ inch (3 mm) above the sides of the pan rim. Pierce the dough all over with a fork. Line the dough with aluminum foil and freeze for 15–30 minutes.

Position a rack in the lower third of the oven and preheat to 375°F (190°C). Place the dough-lined pan on a baking sheet and fill the foil with pie weights or dried beans. Bake until the dough is set and beginning to brown, about 20 minutes.

Meanwhile, make the filling. Bring a medium saucepan three-fourths full of lightly salted water to a boil over high heat. Add the broccoli and cook until the florets are barely tender, about 5 minutes. Drain well, and pat dry with kitchen towels. In a bowl, whisk together the half-and-half, eggs, dill, ½ teaspoon salt, and ¼ teaspoon pepper until combined.

Remove the baking sheet with the tart pan from the oven. Remove the foil and weights. Scatter the broccoli and cheese evenly in the pastry shell. Carefully pour the egg mixture into the shell. Return the sheet to the oven and reduce the oven temperature to 350°F (180°C). Bake until the filling is puffed and golden brown, about 35 minutes. Let cool slightly, then serve.

Change it up Instead of the broccoli, use trimmed asparagus spears, cut into 1-inch (2.5-cm) lengths and blanched in boiling water until tender-crisp, about 3 minutes. You may also wish to substitute Gruyère for the Cheddar cheese.

·STARTERS·

Ranch Dip with Vegetables **65**

Spinach & Artichoke Dip **66**

Deviled Eggs **69**

Fried Green Tomatoes **70**

Jalapeño Poppers **71**

Sausage-Stuffed
Mushrooms **72**

Tomato Bruschetta **75**

Parmesan Toast **75**

Crispy Corn Fritters **76**

Potato Pancakes with
Homemade Applesauce **77**

Fried Calamari with
Spicy Marinara **78**

Roasted Buffalo Wings with
Blue Cheese Dip **81**

What has made ranch dip such a favorite? It starts with a trio of buttermilk, mayonnaise, and sour cream to provide a tangy base, and then is flavored with fresh herbs, onion, and garlic. This delicious combination of ingredients has proven irresistible as a dip for crisp, colorful vegetables.

RANCH DIP WITH VEGETABLES

Makes 6-8 servings

Sour cream, ⅔ cup (5⅓ oz/170 g)

Mayonnaise (page 216 or purchased), ¾ cup (6 fl oz/190 ml)

Buttermilk, ¼ cup (2 fl oz/60 ml)

Yellow onion, 1 small, shredded on the large holes of a box shredder (about 2 tablespoons)

Fresh dill, 2 tablespoons minced

Fresh flat-leaf parsley, 2 tablespoons minced

Garlic, 2 cloves, crushed

Red pepper sauce, 1 teaspoon

Kosher salt, ½ teaspoon

Assorted raw vegetables, such as broccoli and cauliflower florets, cucumber spears, carrots, red endive leaves, radishes, sliced fennel, and celery sticks, and cherry tomatoes, for serving

In a medium bowl, whisk the sour cream, mayonnaise, buttermilk, onion, dill, parsley, garlic, red pepper sauce, and salt together until combined. Cover and refrigerate for at least 1 hour and up to 2 days to blend the flavors.

Transfer the dip to a serving bowl. Serve chilled with the vegetables for dipping.

Lighten it up   Make reduced-calorie version with low-fat mayonnaise and sour cream. (Buttermilk, in spite of its name, is already reduced-fat.) This dip can be thinned with an additional ¼ cup (2 fl oz/60 ml) buttermilk and used as a salad dressing for crisp greens like romaine hearts or iceberg lettuce.

The combination of spinach with artichokes is time-honored, and never better than in this crowd-pleasing dip. Put it out at a party, and watch your guests literally dive in. Use slices of crusty french bread for dunking, or an assortment of crackers or crunchy fresh vegetables.

SPINACH & ARTICHOKE DIP

Makes 6-8 servings

Extra-virgin olive oil, 1 tablespoon, plus more for the baking dish

Yellow onion, ½ cup (2½ oz/75 g) finely chopped

Garlic, 2 cloves, minced

Cream cheese, 8 ounces (250 g), at room temperature

Mayonnaise (page 216 or purchased), 1 cup (8 fl oz/250 ml)

Parmesan cheese, ½ cup (2 oz/60 g) plus 2 tablespoons freshly grated

Romano cheese, ¼ cup (1 oz/30 g) freshly grated, or more Parmesan

Red pepper sauce, 1 teaspoon

Frozen chopped spinach, one 10-ounce (315 g) package thawed

Frozen artichokes hearts, 9 ounces (280 g) thawed, chopped

Baguette, 1, cut into thin slices

Position a rack in the center of the oven and preheat the oven to 350°F (180°C). Lightly oil a 4- to 6-cup (32-fl oz/1-l to 48-fl oz/1.5-l) baking dish.

Heat the oil in a small skillet over medium heat. Add the onion and cook, stirring often, until softened, about 3 minutes. Stir in the garlic and cook until fragrant, about 1 minute more. Transfer to a medium bowl and cool slightly.

Add the cream cheese and mayonnaise to the bowl. Using a silicone or rubber spatula, mash them together to combine. Add the ½ cup (2 oz/60 g) of the Parmesan, the Romano, and hot pepper sauce and mix well.

A handful at a time, squeeze the excess liquid from the spinach, and add the spinach to the cream cheese mixture. Add the artichoke hearts and mix well. Spread in the baking dish and sprinkle with the remaining Parmesan. (The dip can be covered with plastic wrap and refrigerated for up to 1 day.)

Bake until the dip is bubbling and browned, about 30 minutes. Serve hot, with the baguette slices for dipping.

Change it up If you wish, substitute 12 ounces (375 g) fresh baby spinach, cooked for 1 minute in boiling salted water, drained, rinsed and chopped for the frozen spinach. You can also substitute ⅓ cup (1¾ oz/50 g) crumbled goat cheese for the Romano.

A big platter of deviled eggs, stuffed with an herb-flecked, fluffy filling, can round out countless comfort-food menus, from light lunches or suppers to picnics, potlucks, or backyard barbecues. Use homemade mayonnaise in the filling, and your deviled eggs will be legendary among family and friends.

DEVILED EGGS

Makes 4-8 servings

Large eggs, 8

Mayonnaise (page 216 or purchased), ⅓ cup (2¾ oz/80 ml)

Fresh chives, 1 teaspoon minced, plus more for garnish

Fresh tarragon, 1 teaspoon minced, plus more for garnish

Fresh flat-leaf parsley, 1 teaspoon minced, plus more for garnish

Finely grated lemon zest, from 1 lemon

Kosher salt and freshly ground pepper

To hard-boil the eggs, place them in a saucepan just large enough to hold them.

Add cold water to cover by 1 inch (2.5 cm) and bring just to a boil over high heat. Remove the pan from the heat and cover. Let stand for 15 minutes. Drain the eggs, then transfer to a bowl of ice water and let cool completely.

Peel the eggs. Using a sharp, thin-bladed knife, cut each egg in half lengthwise. Remove the yolks, and set the egg white halves aside. Rub the yolks through a coarse-mesh sieve into a bowl. Add the mayonnaise, chives, tarragon, parsley, and lemon zest and whisk together until light and fluffy. Season with salt and pepper and whisk again.

Spoon the yolk mixture into a pastry bag fitted with a medium plain tip. Arrange the egg halves, hollow sides up, on a platter. Pipe the yolk mixture into the egg white halves. (Alternatively, use a teaspoon to fill the egg halves.) Cover lightly with plastic wrap and refrigerate until chilled, about 1 hour. (The eggs can be refrigerated for up to 8 hours before serving.) Sprinkle with additional herbs and serve chilled.

Change it up For a devilishly spicy version, omit the herbs and lemon zest. Stir ½ chipotle chile in adobo, minced, into the mashed egg yolks. Or, go classic and add minced bread-and-butter pickles and 1 teaspoon yellow mustard instead of the herbs and lemon zest.

Southern cooks never pass up an opportunity to serve crispy, tangy, fried green tomatoes. (These are hard, unripened tomatoes, not ripe green-skinned heirloom varieties.) They're great with ham, and make a tasty breakfast topped with crisp bacon, especially if you add the bacon fat to the pan when you fry the tomatoes.

FRIED GREEN TOMATOES

Makes 6-8 servings

All-purpose flour, ¾ cup (4 oz/125 g)

Kosher salt, 2 teaspoons

Freshly ground black pepper, ½ teaspoon

Cayenne pepper, ⅛ teaspoon

Whole milk, 1 cup (8 fl oz/250 ml)

Large eggs, 2

Yellow cornmeal, preferably stone-ground, 1 cup (5 oz/155 g)

Green (unripened) tomatoes, 3 (about 7 ounces/220 g each)

Canola oil, 1 cup (8 fl oz/250 ml)

Rémoulade (page 213) for serving

In a shallow dish, mix together the flour, salt, black pepper, and cayenne pepper. In a second shallow dish, whisk together the milk and eggs until blended. Spread the cornmeal in a third shallow dish. Have ready a baking sheet.

Core the tomatoes and cut crosswise into slices about ¼ inch (6 mm) thick. One at a time, dip the tomato slices into the flour mixture to coat evenly, shaking off the excess. Dip into the egg mixture, letting the excess drip back into the bowl, and then in the cornmeal, patting gently to help it adhere. Transfer to the baking sheet.

Preheat the oven to 200°F (95°C). Set a large wire rack on another rimmed baking sheet and place near the stove. In a large frying pan, heat the oil over medium-high heat until it shimmers. In batches to avoid crowding, add the coated tomato slices to the hot oil and cook until the undersides are golden brown, about 2 minutes. Turn the slices and fry until the other sides are browned, about 2 minutes more. Using a slotted spatula, transfer the tomatoes to the rack and keep warm in the oven while you fry the remaining tomatoes. Serve hot, passing the rémoulade on the side.

Change it up   In New Orleans and elsewhere in the South, you will often see fried green tomatoes topped with a mound of fresh lump crabmeat. Serve with a dollop of Lemon Aioli (page 32).

Often associated as bar food, or purchased in the frozen foods aisle of grocery stores, jalapeño poppers become so much more memorable when made from fresh ingredients and bright green chiles. Whether at the bar or in your home, make sure you have a cold beer on hand to wash away the heat.

JALAPEÑO POPPERS

Makes 6 servings

Applewood-smoked bacon, 2 thick slices, finely chopped

Jalapeño chiles, 12 small

Cream cheese, 4 ounces (125 g), at room temperature

Sharp Cheddar cheese, ½ cup (2 oz/60 g) finely shredded

Monterey Jack cheese, ½ cup (2 oz/60 g) finely shredded

Hot pepper sauce, 1 teaspoon

Kosher salt and freshly ground pepper

Large eggs, 2

Whole milk, 1 tablespoon

Plain fine dried bread crumbs or panko, 1 cup (4 oz/125 g)

Vegetable oil for frying

In a frying pan, fry the bacon over medium heat, stirring occasionally, until crisp and browned, about 5 minutes. Transfer to paper towels to drain.

Using the tip of a paring knife, slit each chile on one side from the stem to the tip, then make a partial cut at the base of the stem, leaving the stem end intact. Gently open up the chile and remove the seeds with the knife or a small spoon.

In a small bowl, mix together the bacon, cream cheese, Cheddar, Monterey Jack, and hot pepper sauce until well blended. Season to taste with salt and pepper. Using a small spoon, fill the chiles with the cheese mixture, dividing it evenly. Close the filled chiles, pressing firmly on the seams so they retain their shape.

In a shall bowl, whisk together the eggs and milk. In a second shallow bowl, stir together the bread crumbs and a pinch each of salt and pepper. One at a time, dip the filled chiles into the egg mixture, allow the excess to drip off, then dip into the bread crumbs, patting gently to help them adhere. Transfer to a baking sheet. Let dry for about 10 minutes, then repeat, dipping the chiles first in the egg mixture and then in the crumbs to form a second coating.

Pour oil to a depth of at least 3 inches (7.5 cm) into a deep, heavy saucepan and heat over medium-high heat to 325°F (165°C) on a deep-frying thermometer. Preheat the oven to 200°F (95°C). Line a rimmed baking sheet with paper towels.

In batches to avoid crowding, add the chiles to the hot oil and deep-fry, stirring occasionally with a wire skimmer, until golden brown, about 6 minutes. Using the skimmer, transfer to paper towels to drain and keep warm in the oven while you fry the remaining chiles. Serve the poppers hot.

These hot appetizers are stuffed high with Italian sausage, bread, and cheese. Look for large "stuffing size" mushrooms at the market and serve them on small plates with cocktail forks, as they may be a bit too large to offer as finger food.

SAUSAGE-STUFFED MUSHROOMS

Makes 4-6 servings

Cremini (baby bella) or large button mushrooms, 12 small, about 1 ounce (45 g) each and 2½ inches (6 cm) across

Extra-virgin olive oil, 5 tablespoons (3 fl oz/ 80 ml), plus more for the baking dish

Italian sweet pork sausages, 8 ounces (250 g), casings removed

Yellow onion, 1 small, finely chopped

Garlic, 1 clove, minced

Coarse fresh bread crumbs, 1½ cups (3 oz/90 g)

Parmesan cheese, 8 tablespoons (2 oz/60 g) freshly grated

Fresh flat-leaf parsley, 1 tablespoon minced

Kosher salt and freshly ground pepper

Remove the stems from the mushrooms, reserving the stems and caps separately. Coarsely chop the stems and set them aside.

In a medium frying pan, heat 1 tablespoon of the oil over medium heat. Add the sausage and cook, stirring occasionally and breaking up the sausage into small bits with the side of a spoon, until the sausage shows no sign of pink, about 5 minutes. Using a slotted spoon, transfer the sausage to a medium bowl.

Add an additional 1 tablespoon of the oil to the skillet. Add the reserved mushroom stems and cook, stirring occasionally, until they begin to give off their juices, about 3 minutes. Stir in the onion and cook stirring occasionally, until it softens, about 3 minutes more. Stir in the garlic and cook until it is fragrant, about 1 minute. Add to the sausage in the bowl. Stir in the bread crumbs, 5 tablespoons (1¼ oz/36 g) of the Parmesan, and the parsley. Mix well and stir in the remaining 3 tablespoons oil to moisten the mixture. Season with the salt and pepper.

Lightly oil a 9-by-13-inch (23-by-33-cm) baking pan. Divide the sausage mixture evenly among the mushroom caps, mounding and pressing the mixture into the caps. Place the stuffed mushrooms into the baking pan and sprinkle with the remaining 3 tablespoons Parmesan. (The mushrooms can be covered with plastic wrap and refrigerated for up to 8 hours before baking.)

Position a rack in the center of the oven and preheat the oven to 350°F (180°C). Bake the mushrooms until they are heated through and the Parmesan cheese has melted and browned, about 30 minutes. Cool slightly and serve.

Lighten it up Substitute turkey Italian sausage for the pork sausage. For a more herbaceous stuffing, substitute 1 teaspoon finely chopped fresh rosemary for the parsley.

Sometimes the most basic of ingredients make the most delicious dishes of all. Of course, to make this dish really shine, seek out the best quality bread, tomatoes, and olive oil you can find. Serve as the first course to a summery, grilled meal.

TOMATO BRUSCHETTA

Makes 4-6 servings

Cherry tomatoes, 1 cup (6 oz/190g), halved

Fresh basil, ¼ cup (¼ oz/7 g), sliced

Extra-virgin olive oil, kosher salt, and freshly ground pepper

Pain au levain

In a bowl, mix the tomatoes, basil, and sprinkle generously with oil, salt, and pepper. Cut the bread into 6 slices, each ½ inch (12 mm) thick.

Heat a heavy grill pan, preferably cast iron, over medium-high heat. Brush the bread with oil and grill, turning once, until toasted on both sides, about 2 minutes. Transfer the grilled bread slices to a serving platter. Mound the tomato salad on top and serve at once.

These simple toasts come together in just 15 minutes, making them a great last-minute appetizer. Simple cheesy toast are delicious on their own, chopped up and tossed in salads and on soups, or fancied up with sliced prosciutto or tapenade.

PARMESAN TOAST

Makes 4-6 servings

Crusty baguette, cut into slices about ½ inch (12 mm) thick

Extra-virgin olive oil, 2 tablespoons

Parmesan cheese, 3 tablespoons freshly grated

Position a rack in the center of the oven and preheat the oven to 400°F (200°C). Place the baguette slices on a baking sheet and brush with the oil. Bake until lightly browned, about 10 minutes. Flip the toasts over and sprinkle each with some of the Parmesan. Continue baking until the cheese is melted and lightly browned, about 5 minutes. Let cool for 1—2 minutes, then serve.

My brothers and I were amazed the first time we saw our father make corn fritters. Peering into the pot—from a safe distance—we watched the dough rounds puff and turn golden-brown in the hot oil. To our family recipe, I've added cilantro and onions, for a slightly Indian flavor.

CRISPY CORN FRITTERS

Makes 6-8 servings

Canola oil for deep-frying

All-purpose flour,
1½ cups (7½ oz/235 g)

Baking powder,
2 teaspoons

Fine sea salt, 1 teaspoon

Whole milk, 1 cup
(8 fl oz/250 ml)

Eggs, 2 large, beaten

Fresh or thawed frozen corn kernels, 1 cup
(6 oz/185 g)

Yellow onion,
2 tablespoons minced

Fresh cilantro,
2 tablespoons minced

Pour oil to a depth of at least 3 inches (7.5 cm) into a large, heavy saucepan, preferably cast iron, and heat over high heat to 350°F (180°C) on a deep-frying thermometer. Preheat the oven to 200°F (95°C). Place a wire rack over a rimmed baking sheet and place near the stove.

While the oil is heating, in a bowl, sift together the flour, baking powder, and salt. Make a well in the center of the flour mixture. In a separate bowl, whisk together the milk and eggs and pour into the well in the flour mixture. Stir just until combined. Gently fold in the corn, onion, and cilantro.

In batches to avoid crowding, add tablespoonfuls of the batter to the hot oil. Deep-fry the fritters until golden brown, turning once at the halfway point, about 3 minutes. Using a wire skimmer or a metal slotted spoon, transfer to the rack and keep warm in the oven while you fry the remaining fritters. Serve at once.

Change it up   For Dad's fritters (see headnote), omit the onions and cilantro. Serve the fritters with maple syrup.

I serve these delicious, crispy-edged potato pancakes the traditional way, with a dollop of sour cream and applesauce. Nearly any apple will work for the sauce—Jonathan, Gala, Fuji, and Golden Delicious are all good—just taste and adjust the amount of sugar as needed.

POTATO PANCAKES WITH HOMEMADE APPLESAUCE

Makes 4 servings

Apples, 2 lb (1 kg), peeled, cored, and cut into cubes

Sugar, 3 tablespoons, or to taste

Finely grated zest of ½ lemon

Fresh lemon juice, 2 tablespoons

Cinnamon, 2-inch (5-cm) stick

Russet potatoes, 2 lb (1 kg), peeled

Yellow onion, 1

Eggs, 2 large, beaten

Dried bread crumbs or matzo meal, 2 tablespoons

Kosher salt and freshly ground pepper

Canola oil, for frying

Sour cream, for serving

Green onions, 2, white and green parts, thinly sliced (optional)

To make the applesauce, in a medium saucepan, combine the apples, ¼ cup (2 fl oz/ 60 ml) water, the sugar, lemon zest and juice, and the cinnamon stick. Bring to a boil over medium heat, stirring occasionally to dissolve the sugar. Cover and reduce the heat to medium-low. Cook, stirring occasionally, until the apples become tender and break down into a sauce, about 15 minutes. Taste and stir in more sugar, if desired. Remove the cinnamon stick. Set aside.

To make the pancakes, preheat the oven to 200°F (95°F). Line a rimmed baking sheet with a wire rack. Line another rimmed baking sheet with paper towels.

Using a food processor fitted with the shredding disk, or the large holes of a box grater-shredder, shred the potatoes and then the onion. A handful at a time, squeeze the potato mixture to remove as much moisture as possible, reserving the liquid in a small bowl and transferring the squeezed potato mixture to a larger bowl. Don't be concerned if the potatoes discolor. Let the liquid stand for a couple of minutes. Pour off and discard the reddish liquid, reserving the potato starch in the bottom of the bowl. Scrape the potato starch into the shredded potato mixture. Add the eggs, bread crumbs, 1 teaspoon salt, and ¼ teaspoon pepper and mix well.

Pour oil to a depth of about ¼ inch (6 mm) into a large, heavy frying pan and heat over medium-high heat until the oil shimmers. For each pancake, spoon about ¼ cup (1 oz/ 30 g) of the potato mixture into the oil and spread into a round. Cook until the bottoms are golden brown, about 2½ minutes. Turn the pancakes and cook until the other sides are brown, about 2½ minutes more. Transfer to the rack and keep warm in the oven. Repeat until all of the potato mixture is used, adding more oil as needed.

Just before serving, transfer the pancakes to the paper towel–lined baking sheet to briefly drain. Serve immediately, with the applesauce and sour cream on the side. Garnish with the green onions, if desired.

Though unsightly in its raw state, calamari is transformed into irresistible finger food after a coating in seasoned flour and a dip in the deep-fryer. A side of spicy, homemade marinara balances out the saltiness of these crispy seafood bites.

FRIED CALAMARI WITH SPICY MARINARA

Makes 4-6 servings

Olive oil, 2 tablespoons

Garlic, 3 cloves, minced

Canned crushed plum tomatoes, 1½ cups (10½ oz/330 g)

Dried oregano, 3 teaspoons

Red pepper flakes, ¼ teaspoon, or more to taste

Canola oil for deep-frying

All-purpose flour, ½ cup (2½ oz/75 g)

Yellow cornmeal, preferably stone-ground, ½ cup (2½ oz/75 g)

Fine sea salt, 1 teaspoon

Cayenne pepper, ¼ teaspoon

Squid (calamari), 1 pound (500 g), cleaned

Fresh flat-leaf parsley, chopped, for garnish

Lemon wedges, for serving

To make the spicy marinara, in a saucepan, heat the olive oil and garlic together over medium-low heat until the garlic softens and is fragrant but not browned, about 3 minutes. Stir in the tomatoes, 1 teaspoon of the oregano, and the red pepper flakes, increase the heat to medium, and bring to a simmer. Return the heat to medium-low and simmer, uncovered, until slightly thickened, about 10 minutes. Remove from the heat and keep warm.

Meanwhile, pour canola oil to a depth of 3 inches (7.5 cm) into a large, heavy saucepan. Heat over high heat to 350°F (180°C) on a deep-frying thermometer. Preheat the oven to 200°F (95°C). Set a large wire rack on a rimmed baking sheet and place near the stove. In a bowl, whisk together the flour, cornmeal, the remaining 2 teaspoons oregano, the salt, and cayenne pepper. Cut the squid bodies crosswise into ¼-inch (6-mm) wide rings; leave the tentacles whole. Toss one-third of the squid rings and tentacles in the flour mixture to coat evenly, shaking off the excess.

In 3 batches, carefully add the coated squid to the hot oil and deep-fry until golden brown, about 2 minutes. Using a wire skimmer, transfer to the rack and keep warm in the oven while you coat and fry the remaining squid.

Spoon the spicy marinara into individual dipping bowls. Transfer the fried calamari to a warmed platter and sprinkle with the parsley. Serve at once, passing the marinara sauce and lemon wedges on the side.

Change it up
This same preparation also works well with shelled shrimp. Dip them first into plain flour and then into beaten eggs before coating them with the flour-cornmeal mixture.

In the finger-licking department, fried chicken has nothing on Buffalo wings. This tempting dish went from a bar snack in upstate New York to a comfort food classic in record time. The original recipe calls for deep-fried wings, but roasting at a high temperature gives equally crisp, lip-smacking results.

ROASTED BUFFALO WINGS WITH BLUE CHEESE DIP

Makes 4-6 servings

Sour cream, ²/₃ cup (5⅓ oz/170 g)

Mayonnaise (page 216 or purchased), ²/₃ cup (5½ fl oz/160 ml)

Blue cheese, 1 cup (5 oz/155 g) crumbled

Scallions, 2 (white and green parts), finely chopped

Garlic, 1 clove, minced

Worcestershire sauce, ½ teaspoon

Freshly ground pepper

Chicken wings, 5 pounds (2.5 kg) (see Note)

Kosher salt, 2 teaspoons

Hot pepper sauce, ½ cup (4 fl oz/125 ml)

Unsalted butter, 4 tablespoons (2 oz/ 60 g), melted

To make the dip, in a medium bowl, whisk the sour cream and mayonnaise together. Add the blue cheese, scallions, garlic, Worcestershire sauce, and ¼ teaspoon pepper and stir well with a wooden spoon, crushing some of the blue cheese into the dip. Cover and refrigerate until ready to use, at least 1 hour or up to 2 days.

Position a rack in the center of the oven and preheat the oven to 425°F (220°C). Line a large rimmed baking sheet, such as a half-sheet pan, with parchment paper.

To make the wings, using a cleaver or a heavy knife, on a chopping board, cut each wing into three pieces between the joints. Discard the wing tips or save for another use (such as stock). Season the wings all over with the salt and 1 teaspoon pepper. Arrange the wings in a single layer on a large rimmed baking sheet, such as a half-sheet pan. Roast, flipping the wings halfway through cooking, until they are crisp and browned, about 45 minutes.

In a large bowl, whisk the hot sauce and melted butter together. Add the wings and mix well to coat the wings. Transfer the wings to a platter. Pour the dip into ramekins or small bowl. Serve the wings at once with the dip and a large bowl to hold the bones.

Note: If you wish, substitute 4½ pounds (2.25 kg) chicken wingettes for the wings. The wingettes don't have to be chopped, but they are often sold frozen, and must be thoroughly defrosted and dried well before roasting.

Change it up Hot sauces vary greatly in their heat levels, colors, and flavors, so the choice of sauce will make a big difference. Serve celery, carrot, or cucumber sticks to dunk into the blue cheese dip. If you want to use a different blue cheese, Roquefort and Gorgonzola work well as substitutes for the Danish variety, although Stilton or Cabrales are a bit too strong.

❖ DINNER ❖

Chicken Piccata 85

Buttermilk Fried Chicken 86

Coq Au Vin 88

Chicken Parmesan 89

Roast Lemon-Thyme Chicken 91

Green Chicken Enchiladas 92

Chicken Potpie 95

Chicken Fricassee with
Mushrooms & Thyme 96

Shepherd's Pie 97

Roast Leg of Lamb with Wine Gravy 98

Grilled Mustard Lamb Chops with
Fresh Mint Sauce 99

Braised Short Ribs with Polenta 101

Pulled Pork Sandwiches 102

Roast Pork with Root Vegetables 104

Real Sloppy Joes 105

Carne Asada Tacos 107

Hearty Beef Stew 108

Texas Beef Chili 109

The Ultimate Cheeseburger 110

Mom's Home-Style Pot Roast 112

Baked Ham 113

Baby Back Ribs 115

Smothered Pork Chops 116

Steak & Mushroom Stroganoff 117

Classic Meatloaf 118

Corned Beef & Cabbage 119

Beef & Broccoli Chow Fun 120

Chicken-Fried Steak with Gravy 122

Porterhouse Steak 123

Spaghetti & Meatballs 125

Potato Gnocchi with Pesto 126

Fettucine Alfredo with
Roasted Cauliflower 128

Mushroom Risotto 129

New York-Style Sausage
& Mushroom Pizza 131

Eggplant Parmesan 132

Lasagna Bolognese 134

Baked Ziti with Sausage 135

Linguine with Clams 137

Fish & Chips 138

Fish Tacos 140

Shrimp & Grits 141

Garlicky Shrimp Scampi 143

One of the many beauties of chicken piccata is its tart lemon sauce, which can also be served with your chosen side dishes—rice and asparagus are particularly good. With very little effort, you can have the dish ready to serve in minutes, and it is a wonderful option to enjoy as a candlelight dinner with a glass of your favorite wine.

CHICKEN PICCATA

Makes 4 servings

Chicken breasts,
4 skinless, boneless, about 6 ounces (185 g) each, halved

Kosher salt and freshly ground pepper

All-purpose flour, ½ cup (2½ oz/75 g)

Extra-virgin olive oil, ¼ cup (2 fl oz/60 ml)

Chicken Stock (page 212) or broth, ½ cup (4 fl oz/125 ml)

Dry white wine, ½ cup (4 fl oz/125 ml)

Finely grated zest of 1 lemon

Fresh lemon juice, ¼ cup (2 fl oz/60 ml)

Nonpareil capers, ¼ cup (2 oz/60 g), rinsed and drained

Unsalted butter, 2 tablespoon, thinly sliced

Fresh flat-leaf parsley, 2 tablespoons, minced, for serving

Using a meat pounder, pound the chicken breasts until they are a uniform ½ inch (12 mm) thick. Sprinkle the chicken evenly with 1½ teaspoons salt and ½ teaspoon pepper. Spread the flour in a shallow bowl. Dip both sides of each chicken breast in the flour, shake off the excess flour and put the breast on a plate.

In a large frying pan, heat the oil over medium heat until the oil is shimmering. In batches to avoid crowding, add the chicken and cook, flipping the chicken halfway through cooking, until golden brown on both sides, about 6 minutes. (The chicken should not be cooked all the way through, as it will finish cooking in the sauce.) Transfer to a plate.

Pour out any fat in the frying pan and wipe it clean with paper towels. Add the stock, wine, lemon zest and juice and bring to a simmer over medium heat. Return all of the chicken breasts and reduce the heat to medium to keep the liquid at a steady simmer. Cook, occasionally turning the chicken, until it shows no sign of pink when pierced in the center with a small, sharp knife, about 2 minutes. Transfer the chicken to a serving platter.

Add the capers to the sauce and simmer gently for 1 minute to heat the capers. Remove the frying pan from the heat. Add the butter and whisk until it melts and lightly thickens the sauce. Season the sauce with salt and pepper. Pour over the chicken and sprinkle the parsley on top. Serve at once.

Change it up Substitute 1½ pounds (750 g) skinless, boneless turkey breast cutlets for the chicken breast halves. The turkey cutlets usually do not have to be pounded. If you wish, omit the capers and parsley, and sprinkle each serving with a generous amount of chopped fresh basil.

Immersing the chicken in the buttermilk brine for several hours gives the chicken loads of flavor and helps keep the meat moist as it fries. The acid in the buttermilk also helps to tenderize the chicken. Serve this dish with a heaping bowl of mashed sweet potatoes in cold weather, or lightly dressed coleslaw on warmer days.

BUTTERMILK FRIED CHICKEN

Makes 4 servings

Buttermilk, 4 cups (32 fl oz/1 l)

Fine sea salt and freshly ground black pepper

Dried oregano, thyme, rosemary, and sage, 2 teaspoons *each*

Granulated garlic, 1 teaspoon

Cayenne pepper, ½ teaspoon

Whole chicken, 1 (about 3½ pounds/1.75 kg)

Canola oil for deep-frying

All-purpose flour, 1⅓ cups (7 oz/215 g)

Baking powder, 1 teaspoon

To make the buttermilk brine, in a large bowl, whisk together the buttermilk and ⅓ cup (2¾ oz/80 g) salt. In a mortar, crush together the oregano, thyme, rosemary, and sage with a pestle (or pulse in a spice grinder) until finely ground. Whisk the ground herbs, garlic, and cayenne pepper into the buttermilk mixture.

Cut the chicken into 2 thighs, 2 drumsticks, 2 wings, and 2 breast halves, reserving the back and giblets for another use. Cut each breast half crosswise to make 4 breast portions, for a total of 10 chicken pieces. Add to the buttermilk brine, making sure that the chicken is submerged. (If it isn't, transfer everything to a smaller bowl.) Cover and refrigerate for at least 4 hours or up to 6 hours.

Pour oil to a depth of at least 3 inches (7.5 cm) into a large, heavy saucepan and heat over high heat to 350°F (180°C) on a deep-frying thermometer. Set a large wire rack on a rimmed baking sheet and place near the stove. Have ready a second rimmed baking sheet. While the oil is heating, in a large bowl, whisk together the flour, baking powder, and ½ teaspoon black pepper. Remove half of the chicken from the buttermilk brine, letting the excess brine drip back into the bowl. Add the chicken to the flour mixture and toss to coat evenly, then transfer to the second baking sheet.

When the oil is ready, in batches to avoid crowding, carefully slip the chicken pieces into the hot oil. The temperature will drop, but adjust the heat to keep the oil bubbling steadily at about 325°F (165°C). Deep-fry the chicken pieces, turning them occasionally with tongs, until they are golden brown and show no sign of pink when pierced at the thickest part, about 12 minutes. Using a wire skimmer, transfer the chicken to the rack to drain. Repeat with the remaining chicken. Serve warm.

Change it up Chicken Maryland is served with cream gravy: After frying the chicken, in a saucepan, heat 2 tablespoons of the cooking oil over medium heat. Whisk in 2 tablespoons flour, simmer for 1 minute, then whisk in 2 cups (16 fl oz/500 ml) heated half-and-half. Bring to a boil, then simmer until thickened, about 5 minutes. Season with salt and pepper. Serve the gravy over the chicken.

Chicken pieces slowly simmered in a rich red wine sauce with mushrooms and small onions until the meat nearly falls from the bones, this French classic is simply one of the most delicious stews around. Use a good-quality light-bodied red, such as Pinot Noir or Beaujolais, that you also enjoy drinking.

COQ AU VIN

Makes 6 servings

Whole chicken, 1 (about 4 pounds/2 kg)

Pancetta, ¼ pound (125 kg), diced

Canola oil, 1 teaspoon

Kosher salt and freshly ground pepper

Unsalted butter, 4 tablespoons (2 oz/60 g)

Cipollini or white boiling onions, 12

Button mushrooms, ½ pound (250 g)

Shallots, ⅓ cup (2 oz/60 g) minced

Garlic, 2 cloves, minced

Cognac, 2 tablespoons

All-purpose flour, ⅓ cup (2 oz/60 g)

Light-bodied red wine, 2 cups (16 fl oz/500 ml)

Chicken Stock (page 212) or broth, 1 cup (8 fl oz/250 ml)

Tomato paste, 2 teaspoons

Fresh thyme, 1½ teaspoons minced

Bay leaf, 1

Wide egg noodles, 1 pound (500 g)

Fresh flat-leaf parsley, for garnish

Preheat the oven to 300°F (150°C). Cut the chicken into 2 drumsticks, 2 thighs, 2 wings, and 2 breast halves, reserving the back and giblets for another use.

In a Dutch oven, brown the pancetta in the oil over medium heat, stirring, until browned, about 8 minutes. Transfer to paper towels to drain, leaving the fat in the pot. Increase the heat to medium-high. Season the chicken pieces with salt and pepper. In batches to avoid crowding, add the chicken pieces to the pot and cook, turning occasionally, until browned on all sides, about 5 minutes per batch. Transfer to a plate.

Add 1 tablespoon of the butter to the pot and melt over medium heat. Add the onions and cook, stirring occasionally, until browned on all sides, about 3 minutes. Transfer to the plate with the chicken. Add 2 tablespoons of the butter to the pot and melt. Quarter the mushrooms. Add the mushrooms and cook, stirring occasionally, until lightly browned, 5—6 minutes. Stir in the shallots and garlic and cook, stirring, until softened, about 2 minutes. Add the Cognac and cook until almost evaporated, 1—2 minutes. Sprinkle in the flour and stir well. Slowly stir in the wine, stock, tomato paste, thyme, and bay leaf and bring to a simmer. Return the chicken pieces to the pot, along with the onions and pancetta. Cover and bake in the oven until the chicken shows no sign of pink when pierced at the bone, 40—45 minutes.

While the chicken is cooking, bring a large pot of salted water to a boil over high heat. Add the egg noodles and stir occasionally until the water returns to a boil. Cook according to the package directions until al dente. Drain the noodles and return to the cooking pot. Add the remaining 1 tablespoon butter and toss to coat.

Discard the bay leaf from the pot. Season with salt and pepper. Divide the noodles among dinner plates and top each serving with the chicken and sauce. Chop the parsley, sprinkle over the servings, and serve at once.

Change it up   For a gluten-free option, the egg noddles can be replaced with roasted fingerling potatoes.

An icon of Italian-American cooking, this version of chicken Parmesan shows the dish at its best—baked chicken with homemade marinara sauce and a topping of fresh mozzarella and Parmesan cheeses. Unlike other versions, the chicken is not breaded, making this a much lighter rendition.

CHICKEN PARMESAN

Makes 4 servings

Extra-virgin olive oil, 3 tablespoons, plus more for the baking dish

Yellow onion, 1, chopped

Garlic, 2 cloves, minced

Canned plum tomatoes, 1 can (28 ounces/875 g), chopped, juices reserved

Dry white wine, ½ cup (4 fl oz/125 ml)

Red pepper flakes, ¼ teaspoon

Chicken breast, 4 skinless, boneless, about 7 ounces (220 g) each, halved

Kosher salt, 1 teaspoon

Freshly ground pepper, ½ teaspoon

Fresh mozzarella, 6 ounces (185 g), cut into thin slices

Parmesan cheese, ½ cup (2 oz/60 g) freshly grated, plus more for serving

Fresh basil, ¼ cup (¾ oz/20 g) finely chopped

To make the tomato sauce, in a medium saucepan, heat 1 tablespoon of the oil over medium heat. Add the onion and cook, stirring occasionally, until softened, about 3 minutes. Stir in the garlic and cook until fragrant, about 1 minute. Stir in the tomatoes with their juices, wine, and red pepper flakes. Bring to a simmer. Reduce the heat to medium low and cook, stirring occasionally, until the sauce has reduced by about one-quarter about 45 minutes.

Preheat the oven to 400°F (200°C). Lightly oil a 13-by-9-inch (33-by-23-cm) baking dish. One at a time, on a work surface, place a chicken breast half between two plastic storage bags. Using the flat side of a meat pounder, pound the chicken until it is about ½-inch (12-mm) thick. Season the chicken with the salt and pepper.

In a large nonstick skillet, heat the remaining 2 tablespoons oil over medium-high heat. In batches to avoid crowding, add the chicken and cook until the underside is lightly browned, about 2 minutes. Flip the chicken and continue cooking just until the other side is lightly browned, about 2 minutes more. The chicken should not be cooked all the way through, as it will finish cooking in the oven. Transfer to a plate.

Pour the hot tomato sauce into the baking dish. Arrange the chicken breast halves in the sauce (the tops should be visible) and top each with an equal amount of mozzarella. Sprinkle the Parmesan over the chicken and sauce. Bake just until the sauce is bubbling around the edges, the mozzarella is melted, and the chicken looks shows no sign of pink when cut in the center with a small sharp knife, 10 to 15 minutes.

Let stand for 5 minutes. Sprinkle the basil over the chicken and sauce. Using a large spoon, divide the chicken breast and sauce among four dinner plates. Serve at once.

Change it up It's not Italian, but shredded Swiss or Gruyère cheese (about an ounce per chicken breast) are both good substitutes for the mozzarella. Instead of pasta, consider cooked rice as a gluten-free side dish.

Few dishes say supper like a beautifully roasted chicken, with burnished, chestnut-colored skin and juicy meat. Surround the chicken with your favorite sturdy vegetables—onions, Brussels sprouts, carrots, and potatoes work well—to roast simultaneously.

ROAST LEMON-THYME CHICKEN

Makes 6-8 servings

Whole roasting chicken,
1 (about 6½ pounds/
3.26 kg)

**Kosher salt and freshly
ground pepper**

Unsalted butter,
4 tablespoons (2 oz/60 g),
at room temperature

**Fresh lemon thyme or
regular thyme,**
2 teaspoons minced plus
2—4 sprigs (optional)

Lemon, 8 thin slices

Olive oil, 1 tablespoon

**Chicken Stock
(page 212) or broth,**
about 2 cups
(16 fl oz/500 ml)

All-purpose flour,
2 tablespoons

Heavy cream, ¼ cup
(2 fl oz/60 ml)

Sprinkle the chicken inside and out with 2 tablespoons salt. Put it into a plastic bag and refrigerate for at least 16 hours and up to 48 hours.

Remove the chicken from the refrigerator 1—2 hours before roasting. Preheat the oven to 425°F (220°C). Rinse the chicken inside and out under cold running water. Pat the chicken very dry with paper towels. In a bowl, mix together the butter and minced thyme. Starting at the cavity, slip your fingers underneath the chicken skin and loosen it all over, being careful not to tear it and reaching as far as possible into the thigh area. Using your fingers, massage the butter under the skin to distribute it as evenly as possible. Slip the lemon slices under the breast skin, 4 slices on each side. Rub the chicken all over with the oil and season with ½ teaspoon pepper. Bend the wing tips and tuck them under the shoulders. Do not truss the chicken.

Place a large, heavy ovenproof frying pan (preferably cast iron) in the oven and heat until very hot, about 5 minutes. Twist a 12-inch (30-cm) length of aluminum foil into a rope, and fashion into a ring. Remove the pan from the oven and carefully place the ring in the pan. Place the chicken, breast side up, on top of the ring. Return the pan to the oven and roast, basting occasionally with the fat in the pan, until an instant-read thermometer inserted into the thickest part of the thigh away from the bone registers 165°F (74°C), about 1 hour and 20 minutes. Transfer the chicken to a platter and let stand for at least 15 minutes before carving.

Discard the foil ring. Pour the pan drippings into a large heatproof liquid measuring cup. Let stand for a few minutes, then spoon off and reserve the fat. Add enough stock to the drippings left in the cup to total 2 cups (16 fl oz/500 ml) liquid.

Return the frying pan to medium heat. Add 2 tablespoons of the reserved fat and whisk in the flour. Let bubble for 1 minute. Gradually whisk in the stock mixture and the cream and bring to a boil. Reduce the heat to low and simmer, whisking frequently, until thickened, about 3 minutes. Season with salt and pepper, add the thyme sprigs, if using, and pour into a sauceboat. Carve the chicken and serve hot, passing the gravy on the side.

These deliciously cheesy enchiladas are stuffed with tender chicken and bathed in a spicy, zesty green tomatillo sauce. Corn tortillas make this Tex-Mex favorite gluten-free. Pile on the sour cream, avocado, and limes, taco-style, as the final touch.

GREEN CHICKEN ENCHILADAS

Makes 4-6 servings

Tomatillos, 1½ pounds (750 g), husks removed

Poblano chilies, 2

Garlic, 5 large cloves, unpeeled

Yellow onions, 2 (1 quartered, 1 sliced)

Olive oil, 2 teaspoons

Ground cumin and dried oregano, 1 teaspoon *each*

Kosher salt

Chicken breasts, 1½ pounds (750 g), on the bone

Farmer's cheese, 1 package (7.5-ounces), crumbled

Freshly ground pepper

Canola oil, ¼ cup (2 fl oz/60 ml), plus more for the baking dish

Corn tortillas, 12

Monterey jack cheese, 1 cup (4 oz/125 g) shredded

Sour cream for serving

Ripe avocado, 1, pitted and cut into ½-inch (12-mm) dice, for serving

To make the enchilada sauce, position the broiler rack about 6 inches (15 cm) from the heat source and preheat the broiler. Place the tomatillos, chilies, and 3 cloves of the garlic on the rack. Brush the onion quarters with the oil and add to the rack. Broil the vegetables until they are browned in spots, about 5 minutes. Remove the garlic. Turn the remaining vegetables on the rack, and continue broiling until the tomatillos turn olive green, the chilies are blackened and blistered, and the onions are singed and tender, about 5 minutes more. Remove from the broiler and let cool. Remove the skins and seeds from the chilies, and peel the garlic. In a blender, purée the tomatillos, chilies, onion, garlic, cumin, oregano, and 1 teaspoon salt.

To make the filling, crush and peel the remaining 2 cloves garlic. Place the chicken in a medium saucepan with the sliced onion and peeled garlic. Add enough water to cover and season with 1 teaspoon salt. Bring to a boil over high heat. Reduce the heat to medium-low and partially cover the saucepan. Simmer for 20 minutes. Let cool in the saucepan for 10 minutes. Remove from the saucepan (you can save the broth for another use) and let cool completely. Remove the chicken meat from the breasts, discarding the bones. Shred the chicken meat. (Do not worry if the chicken is slightly underdone.) Transfer to a medium bowl. Stir in the farmer's cheese, ½ cup (4 oz/125 g) of the enchilada sauce, and season with salt and pepper.

Position a rack in the center of the oven and preheat the oven to 350°F (180°C). Lightly oil a 15-by-10-by-2-inch (38-by-25-by-5-cm) baking dish. Spread ½ cup (4 oz/125 g) of the enchilada sauce in the bottom of the dish.

Heat the oil in a medium frying pan over medium heat. One at a time, fry the tortillas on both sides just until softened, about 10 seconds. Transfer to a plate. For each enchilada, spoon 2 heaping tablespoons of the filling on the bottom third of a tortilla, roll it up, and arrange, seam side down, in the dish. Cover with the remaining sauce and sprinkle with the Monterey jack. Bake until the sauce is bubbling and the cheese is melted and golden, about 30 minutes. Let stand 5 minutes. Serve at once, topping each serving with a dollop of sour cream and some diced avocado.

Both the pastry and the filling here can be made ahead and refrigerated for up to 8 hours before assembling and baking. The finished dish, a bowl of sautéed vegetables, tender chicken, and rich, flaky pie crust, is sure to comfort.

CHICKEN POTPIE

Makes 6 servings

Unsalted butter, 6 tablespoons (3 oz/90 g)

Button mushrooms, ½ pound (250 g), quartered

Leeks, white and pale green parts, 1 cup (4 oz/125 g) chopped

Carrots, ½ cup (2½ oz/75 g) finely diced

Fresh or thawed frozen peas, ⅓ cup (1¾ oz/50 g)

All-purpose flour, ⅓ cup (2 oz/60 g) plus 1 tablespoon

Chicken Stock (page 212) or broth, 4½ cups (36 fl oz/1.1 l)

Dry sherry, ⅓ cup (2.5 fl oz/80 ml)

Fresh tarragon, 2 teaspoons minced

Cooked, shredded chicken (from Chicken Stock, page 212 or purchased rotisserie), 4 cups (24 oz/740 g)

Kosher salt and freshly ground pepper

Double recipe of Flaky Pastry Dough (page 217)

Large egg, 1

To make the sauce and vegetables, in a large frying pan, melt 1 tablespoon of the butter over medium heat. Add the mushrooms and cook, stirring occasionally, until they begin to brown, about 6 minutes. Stir in the leeks and carrots, cover, and cook, stirring occasionally, until the leeks are tender, about 5 minutes. Remove from the heat and stir in the peas.

In a large saucepan, melt the remaining 5 tablespoons (2½ oz/75 g) butter over medium-low heat. Whisk in the flour and let bubble gently for 1 minute. Gradually whisk in the stock and sherry and then the tarragon. Bring to a boil, whisking frequently. Stir in the shredded chicken and the mushroom-leek mixture and season with salt and pepper. Let cool until lukewarm, about 1 hour.

Preheat the oven to 400°F (200°C). Spoon the chicken mixture into six 1½-cup (12 fl oz/375 ml) ovenproof soup crocks or ramekins.

Place the unwrapped dough on a lightly floured work surface and dust the top with flour. (If the dough is chilled hard, let it stand at room temperature for a few minutes until it begins to soften before rolling it out.) Use a knife to cut into six 6-inch (15-cm) squares, discarding the trimmings. Beat the egg with a pinch of salt. Lightly brush each round with the egg. Place 1 round, egg side down, over each ramekin, keeping the pastry taut and pressing it around the ramekin edges to adhere. Place the ramekins on a rimmed baking sheet. Lightly brush the tops with the egg. Bake until the pastry is puffed and golden brown, about 25 minutes.

Transfer each ramekin to a dinner plate and serve.

Lighten it up Instead of flaky pastry dough, cover the ramekins with purchased or homemade phyllo dough.

Fricassee is a close relative to coq au vin, but made with white wine. With its roots in French rustic cooking, it is elegant enough to serve to company. The sauce, earthy with lots of mushrooms and rich with crème fraîche, makes this dish perfect for spooning over a bed of noodles, all the better to sop up every last drop.

CHICKEN FRICASSEE WITH MUSHROOMS & THYME

Makes 4 servings

Whole chicken, 1 (about 3½ pounds/ 1.75 kg)

Kosher salt and freshly ground pepper

Peanut or grape seed oil, 1 teaspoon

Unsalted butter, 4 tablespoons (2 oz/60 g)

Button mushrooms, ¾ pound (375 g), each cut in half lengthwise

Shallots, 2, minced

All-purpose flour, 3 tablespoons

Dry white wine, ¾ cup (6 fl oz/180 ml)

Low-sodium chicken broth or stock, 1½ cups (12 fl oz/375 ml)

Fresh thyme, 4 sprigs

Fresh flat-leaf parsley, 4 sprigs

Crème fraîche, ½ cup (4 fl oz/125 ml)

Fresh chives, 1 tablespoon minced

Cut the chicken into 2 thighs, 2 drumsticks, 2 wings, and 2 breast halves, then season with 1½ teaspoons salt and ½ teaspoon pepper.

In a Dutch oven or other heavy pot with a lid, heat the oil over medium-high heat until very hot but not smoking. Working in batches, add the chicken pieces, skin side down, and cook, turning once or twice, until lightly browned on both sides, about 5 minutes per batch. Transfer to a platter.

Reduce the heat to medium, add the butter, and allow it to melt. Add the mushrooms and sauté until they give off their juices, the juices evaporate, and the mushrooms are sizzling, about 6 minutes. During the last 2 minutes or so, stir in the shallots. Transfer the mixture to a plate.

Return the mushroom mixture to the Dutch oven over medium-low heat, sprinkle with the flour, and mix well. Stir in the wine and broth and bring to a simmer. Gather the thyme and parsley sprigs, tie together with kitchen string, and add to the pot. Return the chicken pieces to the pot. Cover and simmer, stirring the sauce and turning the chicken occasionally, until the chicken shows no sign of pink when pierced with a sharp knife near the bone, 35—40 minutes.

Transfer the chicken to a warmed deep serving dish and tent with aluminum foil. Discard the herb sprigs. Stir the crème fraîche into the pot, raise the heat to medium-high, and bring to a boil. Cook, stirring often, until the sauce is thickened and coats the spoon, about 5 minutes. Taste and adjust the seasonings. Pour the sauce over the chicken, sprinkle with the chives, and serve right away.

The best shepherd's pies start with a simmered lamb stew, flavored with rosemary and a hint of garlic. Capped with creamy mashed potatoes, the topping becomes golden brown in the oven. See the note below for transforming this dish into Rancher's Pie.

SHEPHERD'S PIE

Makes 6 servings

Boneless lamb shoulder,
2 pounds (1 kg)

Kosher salt and freshly ground pepper

Olive oil, 2 tablespoons

Unsalted butter,
8 tablespoons
(4 oz/125 g)

Yellow onion,
1 large, diced

Carrots, 3, diced

Celery, 3 stalks, diced

Garlic, 2 small cloves, minced

All-purpose flour,
6 tablespoons
(2¼ oz/65 g)

Beef Stock (page 212) or broth, 3⅓ cups
(28 fl oz/875 ml)

Dry white wine, ⅔ cup
(5 fl oz/160 ml)

Fresh rosemary,
2 teaspoons minced

Baking potatoes,
3 pounds (1.5 kg)

Heavy cream,
about ⅓ cup (3 fl oz/
80 ml), warmed

Fresh or thawed frozen peas, 1 cup
(5 oz/155 g)

Trim the lamb of excess fat and cut into 1-inch (2.5-cm) cubes. Season with salt and pepper. In a Dutch oven, heat the oil over medium-high heat. In batches to avoid crowding, add the lamb cubes and cook, turning occasionally, until browned on all sides, about 5 minutes per batch. Transfer to a plate.

Add 4 tablespoons (2 oz/60 g) of the butter to the Dutch oven and melt over medium heat. Add the onion, carrots, celery, and garlic, cover, and cook, stirring occasionally, until the carrots are tender-crisp, about 5 minutes. Uncover, sprinkle with the flour, and stir well. Gradually stir in the stock and wine and then the rosemary. Bring to a boil over medium heat, stirring frequently. Return the lamb to the Dutch oven, cover, place in the oven, and cook until the lamb is tender, about 1½ hours.

About 30 minutes before the lamb is ready, preheat the oven to 325°F (165°C). Oil six 2-cup (16 fl oz/500 ml) ovenproof soup crocks or a 3-quart (3-l) baking dish. Peel the potatoes and cut into chunks. In a saucepan, combine the potatoes with salted water to cover, cover the pan, and bring to a boil over high heat. Uncover, reduce the heat to medium, and simmer until the potatoes are tender, 20—25 minutes. Drain well.

Return the potatoes to the pan and stir over medium-low heat for 2 minutes to evaporate the excess moisture. Cut 3 tablespoons of the butter into pieces and add to the potatoes. Using a handheld mixer or a potato masher, whip or mash the potatoes while adding enough cream to create a smooth mixture. Season with salt and pepper.

Season the lamb mixture with salt and pepper, stir in the peas, and pour into the prepared baking dish. Spread the mashed potatoes evenly on top. Cut the remaining 1 tablespoon butter into bits and use to dot the top. Bake until the top is lightly tinged with brown, about 20 minutes. Remove from the oven and let stand for about 5 minutes, then serve hot.

Change it up For Rancher's Pie, substitute 2 pounds (1 kg) boneless beef chuck for the lamb, and fresh thyme for the rosemary. For an extra-rich topping, whip 6 ounces (185 g) of fresh, rindless goat cheese into the potatoes.

Roast lamb on the bone makes a dramatic presentation, and is a favorite main course at holiday feasts. It's simple preparation only requires studding the meat with slivers of garlic and minced rosemary. Make the gravy to serve with the sliced meat and side dishes—which could include a bowl of buttery mashed potatoes.

ROAST LEG OF LAMB WITH WINE GRAVY

Makes 8-10 servings

Garlic, 2 cloves, cut lengthwise into 24 slivers

Extra-virgin olive oil, 1 tablespoon plus 1 teaspoon

Fresh rosemary, 1 tablespoon finely chopped

Leg of lamb, 1, on the bone (about 6½ pounds/3.26 kg), surface fat and membrane trimmed

Kosher salt and freshly ground pepper

Unsalted butter, 5 tablespoons (2½ oz/75 g)

All-purpose flour, ⅓ cup (2 oz/60 g)

Beef Stock (page 212) or broth, 3½ cups (28 fl oz/875 ml)

Dry white wine, ½ cup (4 fl oz/125 ml)

In a small bowl, toss the garlic with 1 teaspoon of the oil, then toss with the rosemary. Using a small, sharp knife, pierce 24 deep slits into the meaty parts of the lamb. Insert a garlic sliver and the rosemary into each slit. Rub the lamb all over with the remaining tablespoon oil and season with 2 teaspoons salt and 1 teaspoon pepper. Let stand at room temperature for 1 hour.

Position a rack in the center of the oven and preheat the oven to 425°F (220°C). Place the lamb in a large roasting pan. Roast for 15 minutes. Reduce the oven temperature to 350°F (180°C) and continue roasting until an instant-read thermometer inserted in the thickest part of the lamb registers 125°–130°F (52–54°C) for medium-rare lamb, 1–1¼ hours. Transfer the roast to a platter and let it stand for 20 minutes before carving.

Pour the drippings from the roasting pan into a small bowl. Let stand 3 minutes, then skim off the fat on the surface. Add the drippings to the stock. Add the butter to the roasting pan and melt over medium heat. Whisk in the flour, scraping up the browned bits in the bottom of the pan, and let the roux bubble for 2 minutes. Whisk in the stock and the wine and bring to a boil. Reduce the heat to medium-low and cook at a steady simmer, whisking often, until thickened and reduced to about 3 cups (24 fl oz/750 ml), about 10 minutes. Season with salt and pepper to taste. Strain the sauce through a wire sieve into a bowl, and transfer to a gravy boat.

To carve, use one hand to hold the lamb by the shank bone. With your other hand, using a sharp carving knife, make vertical several cuts into the meaty part of the lamb, cutting down to the bone. Now make a horizontal cut along the bone to release the slices. Repeat until most of the meat has been carved. Serve at once, with the gravy.

The aroma and flavor of grilled foods brings back memories of lazy summer afternoons and relaxed meals with loved ones. These lamb chops couldn't be easier, with a simple mix of two mustards and garlic. The mint sauce is reminiscent of the familiar green jelly but with a fresh twist that will make it a favorite.

GRILLED MUSTARD LAMB CHOPS WITH FRESH MINT SAUCE

Makes 6 servings

Honey, ¼ cup (3 oz/90 g)

Fresh mint leaves, ½ cup (1 oz/25 g) chopped

White wine vinegar, 3 tablespoons

Kosher salt and freshly ground pepper

Lamb rib chops, 4 double-cut, about 6 ounces/185 g each and cut 1½ inches/ 4 cm thick

Dijon mustard, 3 tablespoons

Stone-ground coarse mustard, 3 tablespoons

Extra-virgin olive oil, 1 tablespoon, plus more for the grill

Garlic, 2 cloves, minced to a paste

To make the mint sauce, in a small saucepan, bring the honey to a simmer over medium heat. Pour into a small bowl. Stir in the mint, vinegar, and season with salt. Let cool completely.

Season the lamb on both sides with 1½ teaspoons salt and 1 teaspoon pepper. In a small bowl, stir the Dijon and coarse mustards with the oil and garlic to combine. Spread the mustard mixture generously on the meaty sides of the lamb chops. Cover and refrigerate for at least 1 and up to 4 hours. Let stand at room temperature for 15 to 30 minutes.

Prepare an outdoor grill for direct cooking over medium-high heat. Brush the grill grate clean and lightly oil the grate. Grill the lamb, with the lid closed, turning once or twice, until an instant-read thermometer inserted through the side into the center of a chop reads 130°F (54°C) for medium-rare meat, about 10 minutes. If the lamb flares up, move the chops to the perimeter of the grill, not directly over the coals (or turn one burner of a gas grill off, and transfer the chops to the grate over the off burner.)

Remove from the grill and let stand for 3 minutes. Serve hot, with the mint sauce passed on the side.

Change it up Add about 2 teaspoons finely chopped fresh green chile, such as jalapeño or serrano, into the mint sauce.

These flavorful short ribs perfectly illustrate how braised meat cooked on the bone can turn out succulent and tender enough to cut with a fork. The bones also enrich the braising liquid, which marries delectably with the cheese-laced creamy polenta. A bold-flavored Syrah or Zinfandel is ideal for the pot and the table.

BRAISED SHORT RIBS WITH POLENTA

Makes 6 servings

Olive oil, 3 tablespoons

Meaty, bone-in, individual-cut short ribs, 6 pounds (3 kg)

Kosher salt, 4 teaspoons

Freshly ground pepper, 1 teaspoon

Yellow onion, 1, chopped

Carrots, 2, diced

Garlic, 6 cloves, chopped

All-purpose flour, ⅓ cup (2 oz/60 g)

Hearty red wine, 2 cups (16 fl oz/500 ml)

Beef Stock (page 212) or broth, 3 cups (24 fl oz/750 ml)

Tomato paste, 2 tablespoons

Fresh rosemary, 1 tablespoon minced

Bay leaf, 1

Whole milk, 1 cup (8 fl oz/250 ml)

Quick-cooking polenta, 1⅓ cups (6⅔ oz/205 g)

Parmesan cheese, ½ cup (2 oz/60 g) freshly grated, plus more for serving

Preheat the oven to 325°F (165°C). In a Dutch oven, heat 2 tablespoons of the oil over medium-high heat. Season the short ribs with 2 teaspoons salt and the pepper.

In batches to avoid crowding, add the short ribs to the pot and cook, turning occasionally, until browned on all sides, 5–6 minutes per batch. Transfer to a plate.

Add the remaining 1 tablespoon oil to the pot and heat. Add the onion and carrots and cook, stirring occasionally, until the onion softens, about 5 minutes. Stir in the garlic and cook until fragrant, about 1 minute. Sprinkle in the flour and stir well. Slowly stir in the wine, then the stock. Stir in the tomato paste, rosemary, and bay leaf. Return the short ribs to the pot. The short ribs should be barely covered with liquid. If not, add hot water as needed. Bring the liquid to a boil. Cover the pot, place in the oven, and cook, moving the position of the ribs every 45 minutes or so to be sure that they are covered with liquid and are cooking evenly, until very tender, about 2½ hours. Transfer the ribs to a deep serving platter (don't worry if the meat separates from the bones), and tent with aluminum foil to keep warm.

Let the cooking liquid stand for 5 minutes. Skim off the fat from the surface and discard. Bring to a boil over high heat. Cook, stirring, until reduced by about one-fourth, about 10 minutes. Discard the bay leaf. Return the short ribs to the pot.

Just before serving, make the polenta: In a heavy saucepan, bring 3 cups (24 fl oz/750 ml) water, the milk, and the remaining 2 teaspoons salt to a boil over high heat. Slowly whisk in the polenta and reduce the heat to medium-low. Cook, whisking often, until the polenta is thick, about 2 minutes. Stir in the ½ cup (2 oz/60 g) Parmesan. Divide the polenta among warmed deep serving bowls, top with the ribs and sauce and serve at once.

In the Carolinas, "real" barbecue is languidly cooked in a smoker with hickory wood, but more people likely make it this way, in the oven. It takes forever, but what a payoff: a mountain of meltingly tender meat, perfect for a big family gathering or for when you want leftovers for other meals down the road.

PULLED PORK SANDWICHES

Makes 10 sandwiches

Bone-in pork shoulder, 1 (about 7½ pounds/ 3.75 kg)

Sweet paprika, preferably Hungarian or Spanish, 2 teaspoons

Dried thyme, ¾ teaspoon

Dried oregano, ¾ teaspoon

Kosher salt and freshly ground black pepper

Cayenne pepper, ⅛ teaspoon

Cider vinegar, 2½ cups (20 fl oz/625 ml)

Yellow onion, 1, chopped

Garlic, 5 cloves, minced

Light brown sugar, ¼ cup (2 oz/60 g) lightly packed

Ketchup (page 215 or purchased), ¼ cup (2 oz/60 g)

Red pepper flakes, 1 teaspoon

Canola oil, ⅓ cup (3 fl oz/80 ml)

Green cabbage, 1 small head, shredded

Soft sandwich buns, 10, split

Position a rack in the lower third of the oven and preheat to 325°F (165°C). Cut the rind off the pork shoulder, leaving a thin layer of fat. Using a sharp knife, score the fat in a crosshatch pattern, creating 1-inch (2.5-cm) diamonds. Mix together the paprika, thyme, oregano, 2 teaspoons salt, ½ teaspoon black pepper, and the cayenne pepper. Sprinkle the mixture evenly over the pork and rub it in. Place the pork in a large Dutch oven and add ½ cup (4 fl oz/125 ml) of the vinegar, the onion, and two-thirds of the garlic. Cover and bake, turning the pork every hour or so, until it is fork-tender and an instant-read thermometer inserted in the thickest part away from the bone registers at least 190°F (90°C), 5–6 hours.

Meanwhile, to make the barbecue sauce, in a bowl, whisk together the remaining 2 cups (16 fl oz/500 ml) vinegar, the remaining garlic, the sugar, ketchup, and red pepper flakes. The sauce will be thin. Measure out ¼ cup (2 oz/60 g) sauce, then transfer the remaining sauce to a covered container and set aside at room temperature. To make the coleslaw, in a bowl, whisk together the ¼ cup (2 oz/60 g) barbecue sauce and the oil. Add the cabbage and mix to coat evenly. Season with salt and pepper. Cover and refrigerate for at least 2 hours to allow the cabbage to soften and the flavors to mingle.

When the pork is ready, transfer it to a carving board and tent with aluminum foil to keep warm. Let stand for at least 20 minutes. Meanwhile, skim the fat from the cooking liquid, then boil the liquid over high heat until reduced to about ¾ cup (6 fl oz/180 ml). Using 2 forks, pull the pork shoulder into shreds. (Once the pork has been pulled apart into large chunks, it may be easier to use a knife to help shred the meat.) Transfer to a serving bowl and moisten with the reduced cooking liquid. To serve, heap the pulled pork and a spoonful of the slaw onto the bottom half of each bun and cover with the bun top. Serve at once, passing sauce on the side.

Change it up   If you don't have a large Dutch oven, cook the pork in a roasting pan, tightly covered with aluminum foil. For a real treat, add a layer of pulled pork to your favorite grilled cheese sandwich.

There are few aromas more satisfying than roasting pork wafting through the house on a weekend afternoon. This version, with root vegetables browned in the roast's juices, is inspired by French country cooking, with a fresh herb rub and a white wine pan sauce. Carve the pork and serve it with the sauce poured on top.

ROAST PORK WITH ROOT VEGETABLES

Makes 8 servings

Extra-virgin olive oil, 3 tablespoon

Pork loin, one 5-pound (2.5-kg), with rib bones, chine bone sawed by the butcher, and excess fat trimmed

Fresh rosemary, 2 teaspoons finely chopped

Fresh sage, 2 teaspoons finely chopped

Fresh thyme, 2 teaspoons finely chopped

Kosher salt and freshly ground pepper

Red-skinned potatoes, 2 pounds (1 kg), scrubbed, cut into 1-inch (2.5-cm) chunks

Carrots, 1 pound (500 g), cut into 1-inch (2.5-cm) chunks

Parsnips, 12 ounces (375 g), peeled, cut into 1-inch (2.5-cm) chunks

Dry white wine, 1 cup (8 fl oz/250 ml)

Unsalted butter, 2 tablespoons, thinly sliced

Brush the pork roast all over with 1 tablespoon of the oil. In a small bowl, mix the rosemary, sage, and thyme with 2 teaspoons salt and 1 teaspoon pepper. Season the pork all over with the herb mixture. Let stand at room temperature for 1 hour.

Preheat the oven to 425°F (220°C). Place the roast, meaty side up, in a very large roasting pan. Roast for 15 minutes. Reduce the oven temperature to 350°F (180°C), and roast for 30 minutes more.

In a large bowl, toss the potatoes, carrots, and parsnips with the remaining 2 tablespoons oil. Spread around the pork. Continue roasting until the internal temperature of the pork reaches 145°F (63°C) on an instant-read thermometer, about 40 minutes more. Transfer the pork to a carving board and let stand while finishing the vegetables and sauce. (There is no need to cover the pork.)

Using a large metal spatula, flip the vegetables in the pan. Increase the oven temperature to 450°F (230°C). Roast the vegetables until they are lightly browned and tender, about 10 minutes. Season with salt and pepper to taste. Transfer the vegetables to a bowl and tent with aluminum foil to keep warm.

Place the roasting pan over high heat. Add the wine and bring to a boil, scraping up the browned bits in the pan with a wooden spoon. Boil until the liquid is reduced by half, about 3 minutes. Remove the pan from the heat. Add the butter and whisk until it is absorbed into the sauce. Season with salt and pepper. Carve the pork and transfer the meat to a platter. Pour the sauce on top. Serve immediately, with the vegetables.

Change it up   Other root vegetables, such as sweet potatoes, celery root, turnips, and parsley root, can substitute for the potatoes, carrots, and parsnips.

The poor sloppy Joe has gotten a bad rap. Perhaps the uninspired versions served by overworked school cafeteria staffers dulled whatever luster it ever possessed. Here's a recipe that returns the sloppy Joe to its rightful position as a dish to cherish when you want a quick and unpretentious supper on a bun.

REAL SLOPPY JOES

Makes 6 sandwiches

Canola oil, 1 tablespoon

Yellow onion, 1, diced

Celery, 1 stalk, diced

Green bell pepper, ¼ cup (1¼ oz/40 g), finely diced

Ground beef, 1½ pounds (750 g)

Tomato sauce, 1 cup (8 oz/250 g)

Ketchup-style chili sauce, ½ cup (4 oz/125 g)

Worcestershire sauce, 1 tablespoon

Dijon mustard, 1 tablespoon

Cider vinegar, 1 tablespoon

Light brown sugar, 1 tablespoon firmly packed

Kosher salt, 1 teaspoon

Freshly ground pepper, ¼ teaspoon

Sesame-seed sandwich buns, 6, split

In a large frying pan, heat the oil over medium heat. Add the onion, celery, and bell pepper and cook, stirring occasionally, until the onion softens, about 5 minutes. Add the beef and increase the heat to medium-high. Cook, stirring and breaking up the beef with a wooden spoon, until it is no longer pink, about 10 minutes. Stir in ¼ cup (2 fl oz/60 ml) water, the tomato sauce, chili sauce, Worcestershire sauce, mustard, vinegar, sugar, salt, and pepper and bring to a simmer. Reduce the heat to medium-low and simmer, stirring frequently, for about 20 minutes to blend the flavors.

Toast the buns. Place the bottom halves of the buns, cut side up, on warmed individual plates and top with the beef mixture, dividing it equally. Cover with the bun tops and serve right away.

Lighten it up Sloppy Joes are just as good when made with ground turkey or ground chicken. Some cooks like to add 1–2 cups (7 oz/220 g–14 oz/440 g) cooked kidney or pinto beans to the beef mixture just before it is ready. Or, you can top the beef mixture with thin slices of Cheddar cheese before covering with the bun tops.

These authentic tacos—boldly seasoned slices of grilled steak and creamy guacamole rolled up in warm corn tortillas—are bursting in flavor. The guacamole can be replaced with plain slices of fresh avocado and fresh cilantro and lime juice sprinkled directly on the tacos. Grilled fresh corn makes for a great side dish.

CARNE ASADA TACOS

Makes 6 servings

TACOS

Chili powder, 2 teaspoons

Kosher salt, 1 teaspoon

Dried oregano, 1 teaspoon

Ground cumin, 1 teaspoon

Granulated garlic, ½ teaspoon

Skirt steak, 1½ pounds (750 g), cut into 2 or 3 pieces

CREAMY GUACAMOLE

Ripe avocado, 1, pitted, peeled, and diced

Sour cream, ¼ cup (2 oz/60 g)

Fresh lime juice, 1 tablespoon

Kosher salt

Fresh cilantro, 3 tablespoons chopped

Corn tortillas, 12

Lime, 1, cut into wedges

To prepare the steak, mix together the chili powder, salt, oregano, cumin, and garlic. Sprinkle the mixture on both sides of the steak and rub it into the meat. Let stand at room temperature while you make the guacamole and ready the grill.

To make the guacamole, halve, pit, peel, and coarsely dice the avocado. In a bowl, combine the avocado, sour cream, and lime juice, and mash the avocado with a fork to form a chunky purée. Season with salt and stir in the cilantro. Place a piece of plastic wrap directly on the surface of the guacamole and let stand at room temperature while you prepare the grill.

Prepare a grill for direct-heat cooking over high heat. Lightly oil the cooking grate.

Place the steaks on the grill and cover. Grill until the undersides are browned, about 2½ minutes. Turn the steaks and grill until the second sides are browned and the meat feels slightly resilient when pressed in the center, about 2½ minutes more for medium-rare. (Skirt steak is too thin to test with an instant-read thermometer, so use this "touch test" instead.) Transfer to a carving board, tent with aluminum foil to keep warm, and let stand for 5 minutes.

Grill the tortillas, turning once, until they are warm and pliable, about 1 minute. Wrap in a large cloth napkin or kitchen towel to keep warm. With the carving knife held at a slight diagonal, cut the steaks across the grain into thin slices. Transfer to a bowl, adding any juices from the board.

Serve the steak, guacamole, and tortillas at once, passing the lime wedges on the side. Allow diners to fill their own tacos.

Change it up You can add all sorts of ingredients to these tacos to make them your own: fresh tomato salsa, shredded lettuce, dollops of crema or sour cream, or crumbled cotija or shredded Monterey Jack cheese. You can also opt for flour tortillas over corn.

Adding lots of vegetables to the pot adds flavor and nutrition to the velvety sauce. For a richer sauce, substitute 1½ cups (12 fl oz/375 ml) hearty red wine, such as Syrah or Zinfandel, for an equal amount of the beef stock. Pick a bottle you enjoy enough to drink with the finished meal.

HEARTY BEEF STEW

Makes 6 servings

Boneless beef chuck,
3 pounds (1.5 kg)

Applewood-smoked bacon, 4 thick
slices, chopped

Canola oil, 2 tablespoons

Kosher salt and freshly ground pepper

Yellow onion, 1, chopped

Carrots, 3, cut into chunks

Celery, 3 stalks, cut into
½-inch (12-mm) lengths

Garlic, 2 cloves, chopped

Unsalted butter,
2 tablespoons

All-purpose flour,
6 tablespoons
(2¼ oz/65 g)

Beef Stock (page 212) or broth, 4 cups (2 fl oz/1 l)

Tomato paste,
2 tablespoons

Fresh flat-leaf parsley,
1 tablespoon chopped,
plus more for garnish

Fresh thyme and rosemary, 1 teaspoon
each, minced

Bay leaf, 1

Red-skinned potatoes,
1¼ pounds (625 g)

Position a rack in the lower third of the oven and preheat to 325°F (165°C). Cut the beef into 1½-inch (4-cm) cubes and set aside. In a large Dutch oven, cook the bacon in the oil over medium heat, stirring occasionally, until the bacon is crisp and browned, about 7 minutes. Using a slotted spoon, transfer to paper towels to drain and set aside. Pour the fat into a heatproof bowl. Return 2 tablespoons of the fat to the pot and heat over medium-high heat. Season the beef cubes with salt and pepper. In batches to avoid crowding, add the beef and cook, stirring occasionally, until browned on all sides, about 5 minutes per batch. Transfer the beef to a plate.

Add another 2 tablespoons of the fat to the pot and heat over medium heat. Add the onion, carrots, celery, and garlic and cook, stirring occasionally, until the onion softens, about 5 minutes. Stir in the butter and let it melt. Sprinkle with the flour and stir well. Gradually stir in the stock, and then stir in the tomato paste, the 1 tablespoon parsley, thyme, rosemary, and bay leaf. Return the beef to the pot and bring to a boil. Cover, place in the oven, and cook for 1½ hours.

Cut the unpeeled potatoes into 1-inch (2.5-cm) cubes, add them to the pot, stir, re-cover, and continue cooking until both the meat and potatoes are tender, about 45 minutes more. Season the stew with salt and pepper. Serve at once, garnished with parsley and the reserved bacon.

Lighten it up   If you want to add more vegetables to this dish, sauté ½ pound (250 g) cremini mushrooms, quartered, in 2 tablespoons olive oil over medium heat until browned, about 5 minutes, and add them to the stew with the potatoes.

What makes chili Texan? Most Lone Star chili masters eschew beans and tomatoes. To them, chili is all about meat—beef only—and the chile seasoning. But, if you want to keep your bowl balanced and delicious, heap on the vegetable toppings and serve with a square of naturally whole-grain cornbread—just don't tell the Texans!

TEXAS BEEF CHILI

Makes 8 servings

Whole cumin seeds,
2 teaspoons

Pure ancho chile powder,
¼ cup (1 oz/30 g)

Spanish smoked paprika,
1 tablespoon

Dried oregano,
2 teaspoons

Boneless beef chuck roast, 4 pounds (2 kg)

Kosher salt and freshly ground pepper

Olive oil, 3 tablespoons

Yellow onion, 1 large, chopped

Jalapeño, 1, seeds and ribs removed, chopped

Red bell pepper, 1 large, seeded and chopped

Garlic, 4 cloves, chopped

Lager beer, 1½ cups (12 fl oz/375 ml)

Beef Stock (page 212), broth, or water, 1 cup (8 fl oz/250 ml)

Yellow cornmeal, 2 tablespoons

Shredded Cheddar cheese, chopped red onions, sour cream, and minced jalapeño chiles, for serving

Heat a frying pan over medium heat. Add the cumin seeds and heat, stirring often, until toasted (you may see a wisp of smoke), about 1 minute. Transfer to a mortar and finely grind with a pestle (or use a spice grinder). Transfer to a bowl and add the ancho chile powder, paprika, and oregano. Mix well and set aside.

Cut the beef into ½-inch (12-mm) cubes. Season with salt and pepper. In a Dutch oven, heat 2 tablespoons of the oil over medium-high heat. In batches to avoid crowding, add the beef cubes and cook, turning occasionally, until browned, about 5 minutes per batch. Transfer to a plate.

Add the remaining 1 tablespoon oil to the pot. Add the onion, jalapeño, bell pepper, and garlic and reduce the heat to medium. Cover and cook, stirring occasionally, until the onion softens, about 5 minutes. Uncover, add the spice mixture, and stir well for 30 seconds. Stir in the beer and stock. Return the beef to the pot, cover, and reduce the heat to low. Simmer until the beef is fork-tender, 1½–2 hours.

Remove the chili from the heat and let stand for 5 minutes. Skim off any fat that rises to the surface. Return the pot to medium heat and bring to a simmer. Transfer about ½ cup (4 fl oz/125 ml) of the cooking liquid to a small bowl, add the cornmeal, and whisk well. Stir into the chili and cook until lightly thickened, about 1 minute.

Season with salt and pepper. Spoon the chili into warmed bowls and serve hot, with bowls of Cheddar, onions, sour cream, and jalapeños on the side for sprinkling on top.

Lighten it up At the risk of making some Texans hoppin' mad, add 1 cup (7 oz/ 220 g) cooked kidney or pinto beans to your chili and heat through just before serving. You can also add 1 cup (8 oz/250 g) or so of chopped canned tomatoes. Ancho chiles are relatively mild, so if you want a hotter chili, add some cayenne pepper. This chili is excellent served with Cornbread (page 172) or warmed tortillas to capture every last bit of the brick-red sauce.

Making a burger sounds like a simple endeavor, but to make a truly great one, each of the ingredients you use, from the beef to the bun to the tomato, should be of the best quality. The better the beef, the better the burger, so use organic free-range beef if possible. Don't use extra lean beef—burgers need a little fat to stay juicy.

THE ULTIMATE CHEESEBURGER

Makes 4 burgers

Ground beef round, 1½ pounds (750 g)

Yellow onion, 1, plus 3 tablespoons minced

Worcestershire sauce, 1 tablespoon

Kosher salt and freshly ground pepper

Hamburger buns, 4, split

Unsalted butter, 2 tablespoons, melted

Canola oil for brushing

Cheddar cheese, 4 slices

Ripe beefsteak or heirloom tomato, 1 large, sliced

Butter or red-leaf lettuce, 4 leaves

Ketchup (page 215 or purchased) for serving

Mayonnaise (page 216 or purchased) for serving

Bread-and-butter pickles for serving

Prepare a grill for direct-heat cooking over medium-high heat. In a bowl, combine the beef, the 3 tablespoons minced onion, Worcestershire sauce, 1½ teaspoons salt, and ¾ teaspoon pepper and mix gently with your hands just until combined. Divide the mixture into 4 equal portions, and shape each portion into a patty about ¾ inch (2 cm) thick. Brush the cut sides of each bun with the butter.

Cut the whole onion into rounds about ¼ inch (6 mm) thick, but don't separate the rings. Brush the rounds with oil and season with salt and pepper. Lightly oil the cooking grate. Grill the onion rounds, turning once, until slightly softened and grill marks are visible, about 3 minutes on each side. Grill the patties for about 3 minutes, then turn and place a cheese slice on top of each patty. Cook on the second sides for an additional 3 minutes for medium-rare, or until done to your liking. During the last 2 minutes of cooking the patties, place the buns, cut sides down, on the grill and toast until lightly browned.

Transfer the buns, cut side up, to plates. Place a patty on the bottom half of each bun and top with the grilled onions, tomato slices, and lettuce. Serve at once, allowing diners to add ketchup, mayonnaise, and pickles as desired.

Change it up   Mix it up by changing the toppings: Use crumbled blue cheese instead of Cheddar, or Beer-Battered Onion Rings (page 147) instead of grilled onions. And sautéed mushrooms or crisp bacon slices are welcome additions to any burger.

In this recipe, thickly sliced onions, paprika, and bacon fat boost the flavor. But, carrots, parsnips, or sweet potatoes are also great for transforming a modest chuck roast into a flavorful meal. You'll have lots of sauce from this recipe, so make Buttery Mashed Potatoes (page 158) for soaking it up.

MOM'S HOME-STYLE POT ROAST

Makes 4-6 servings

Yellow onions, 3

Beef chuck roast, 1 (about 2½ pounds/ 1.25 kg)

Kosher salt and freshly ground pepper

All-purpose flour, ¼ cup (½ oz/45 g)

Rendered bacon fat or canola oil, 3 tablespoons

Garlic, 4 cloves, chopped

Sweet paprika, preferably Hungarian or Spanish, 1 teaspoon

Beef Stock (page 212) or broth, 1½ cups (12 fl oz/375 ml)

Canned plum tomatoes, 1½ cups (15 oz/460g), drained and chopped

Fresh flat-leaf parsley, 2 tablespoons chopped, plus more for garnish

Halve the onions through the stem, and cut the halves into ½-inch (12-mm) thick half-moons. Set aside. Season the chuck roast with ¾ teaspoon salt and ½ teaspoon pepper. Spread the flour on a plate. Coat the roast with the flour, shaking off the excess.

In a Dutch oven, heat 2 tablespoons of the bacon fat over medium-high heat. Add the roast and cook, turning occasionally, until browned on both sides, about 5 minutes total. Transfer to a plate.

Add the remaining 1 tablespoon bacon fat to the pot and heat over medium-high heat. Add the onions, cover, and cook, stirring occasionally, until the onions soften, about 6 minutes. Stir in the garlic and paprika and cook until the garlic is fragrant, 1—2 minutes. Add the stock, tomatoes, and 2 tablespoons parsley and stir. Return the beef to the pot, nestling it in the onions. Bring the liquid to a boil, reduce the heat to medium-low, cover, and simmer until the beef is fork-tender, about 2 hours.

Transfer the pot roast to a deep serving platter. Season the onion mixture with salt and pepper. Skim off any fat from the surface. Spoon the onion mixture around the roast and sprinkle with more parsley. Serve at once.

Change it up To make beef paprikash, simply add sour cream to the sauce. Transfer the pot roast to a platter and skim the fat from the sauce as directed. Stir 1 cup (8 oz/250 g) sour cream into the sauce and cook just until it is heated through; do not allow to boil. Season with salt and pepper. Pot roast also makes excellent hot sandwiches. Slice the roast and serve it along with plenty of the saucy onions on crusty rolls.

Ham owes its popularity not only to its smoky-salty flavor but also to its talent for feeding a lot of people with very little effort. This recipe, with a simple ginger and orange glaze, is no exception. Whip up a batch of Buttermilk Biscuits (page 171) and a dish of Rich Scalloped Potatoes (page 153) for the ultimate comfort food menu.

BAKED HAM

Makes 12 servings

Shank-end smoked ham,
1 (about 5 pounds/2.5 kg)

Unsalted butter,
1 tablespoon

Fresh ginger,
2 tablespoons peeled
and minced

**Dark rum, bourbon, or
fresh orange juice,**
3 tablespoons

Bitter orange marmalade,
½ cup (5 oz/155 g)

Dijon mustard,
1 tablespoon

Position a rack in the lower third of the oven and preheat to 325°F (165°C). Line a roasting pan with aluminum foil, and place a roasting rack in the pan.

Using a sharp knife, score the fat on the ham in a crosshatch pattern, creating 1½-inch (4-cm) diamond shapes. Place the ham, flat side down, on the rack in the roasting pan. Add 2 cups (16 fl oz/500 ml) water to the pan and cover loosely with aluminum foil. Bake until an instant-read thermometer inserted in the thickest part of the ham away from the bone registers 125°F (52°C), about 1¼ hours.

Meanwhile, make the glaze. In a small saucepan, melt the butter over medium heat.

Add the ginger and cook, stirring occasionally, until it softens, about 2 minutes. Add the rum and boil until it is reduced by half, about 2 minutes. Stir in the marmalade and mustard and bring to a boil, then remove from the heat and set aside to cool.

Remove the ham from the oven and discard the foil on top. Increase the oven temperature to 400°F (200°C). Spread the glaze all over the ham, forcing some of it into the scoring marks. Return to the oven and bake, uncovered, until the glaze melts onto the ham, about 15 minutes.

Transfer the glazed ham to a carving board. Let stand for 15 minutes, then carve into slices parallel to the bone. Serve hot or warm.

Change it up After the ham is sliced, be sure to save the ham bone for adding to your favorite recipe for split pea soup or a big pot of beans. Chop the leftover ham and stir it into the soup or beans, too.

Folks can't eat these tasty ribs without licking their fingers. The double-cooking method—first rubbed with pungent spices and slowly baked, then finished outdoors on a hot grill with a zesty glaze—results in extra flavorful and tender meat that will pull away from the bone with the slightest tug of the teeth.

BABY BACK RIBS

Makes 4—6 servings

Baby back ribs,
2 racks (about
5 pounds/2.5 kg total)

Kosher salt, 2 teaspoons

**Spanish smoked
paprika,** 1 teaspoon

Dried oregano,
1 teaspoon

Dried thyme, 1 teaspoon

Granulated garlic,
½ teaspoon

Onion powder,
½ teaspoon

Freshly ground pepper,
½ teaspoon

**Ketchup-style chili
sauce,** ½ cup
(4 oz/125 ml)

**Peach or apricot
preserves,** ½ cup
(5 oz/155 g)

**Unsulfured
dark molasses,**
2 tablespoons

Cider vinegar,
1 tablespoon

Dijon mustard,
1 tablespoon

Hot pepper sauce,
½ teaspoon

Canola oil for grilling

Preheat the oven to 350°F (180°C). Cut each rib rack into 2 or 3 sections. Mix together the salt, paprika, oregano, thyme, granulated garlic, onion powder, and pepper. Sprinkle the mixture on both sides of the ribs and rub it into the meat.

Arrange the ribs, overlapping slightly if necessary, in a large roasting pan. Cover tightly with aluminum foil, place in the oven, and cook for 30 minutes. Remove the foil, turn the ribs, and return to the oven. Continue cooking until the ribs are tender and browned, about 30 minutes more.

Meanwhile, make the sauce. In a small saucepan, stir together the chili sauce, peach preserves, molasses, vinegar, mustard, and hot pepper sauce and bring to a simmer over medium-low heat. Remove from the heat and set aside.

While the ribs are cooking, prepare a grill for direct-heat cooking over medium-high heat. Lightly oil the cooking grate. Brush both sides of the ribs with the sauce. Place on the grill, cover, and cook, turning once, until shiny and glazed, about 3 minutes per side. (Alternatively, increase the oven temperature to 425°F (220°C). Pour off the fat in the roasting pan, then return the ribs to the pan. Brush the ribs with some of the sauce and cook until the ribs are shiny and glazed, about 5 minutes. Turn, brush with more of the sauce, and cook to glaze the other side, about 5 minutes more.)

Transfer the ribs to a carving board and let stand for 5 minutes. Cut between the bones into individual ribs, heap on a platter, and serve with any remaining sauce.

Change it up Pork spareribs are also excellent prepared with this oven-barbecue method. They are larger, meatier, and a little tougher than baby back ribs, so they will take about 45 minutes of covered baking, another 45 minutes uncovered, and a final 15 minutes for the glazing.

In this beloved southern recipe, meaty bone-in pork chops are literally smothered in vegetables and stock, then simmered until the vegetables have melted into a sauce tailor-made for spooning over rice. This is a purposely mellow version, so if you crave spicy food, jazz it up with a teaspoon or so of Cajun seasoning.

SMOTHERED PORK CHOPS

Makes 4 servings

Center-cut bone-in pork loin chops, 4, each about 1 inch (2.5 cm) thick

Kosher salt and freshly ground pepper

Canola oil, 2 tablespoons

Unsalted butter, 2 tablespoons

Yellow onion, 1 large, chopped

Green bell pepper, 1 small, seeded and diced

Celery, 3 stalks, diced

Green onions, 4, white and green parts, chopped

Garlic, 3 cloves, minced

Fresh thyme, 1 teaspoon minced

All-purpose flour, 3 tablespoons

Chicken Stock (page 212) or broth, 2½ cups (20 fl oz/ 625 ml)

Heavy cream, ¼ cup (2 fl oz/60 ml)

Hot pepper sauce

Steamed rice for serving

Season the pork chops with salt and pepper. In a very large frying pan, heat the oil over medium-high heat. Add the chops to the pan and cook until the undersides are browned, about 3 minutes. Turn and brown the second sides, about 3 minutes more. Transfer to a plate.

Add the butter to the pan and reduce the heat to medium. When the butter has melted, add the onion, bell pepper, celery, green onions, and garlic and stir with a wooden spoon to loosen any browned bits in the pan. Cover and cook, stirring occasionally, until the vegetables are tender, about 8 minutes. Stir in the thyme. Sprinkle in the flour and stir well. Gradually stir in the stock and bring to a simmer.

Return the pork chops to the pan and reduce the heat to medium-low. Cover and simmer until the pork shows no sign of pink when pierced at the bone, about 20 minutes. Transfer the pork chops to a deep serving platter and tent with aluminum foil to keep warm.

Stir the cream into the gravy in the pan and bring to a boil. Cook until thickened, about 1 minute. Season to taste with salt and hot pepper sauce. Pour the gravy over the pork, and serve at once with the steamed rice.

Lighten it up Chicken breasts are another excellent candidate for the smothered treatment. Sear boneless, skinless chicken breast halves for about 2 minutes on each side, then simmer them in the sauce for about 15 minutes.

Tender chunks of steak, sweet shallots, loads of sautéed mushrooms, and an outrageously rich sour cream sauce make up this warming dish, named after a nineteenth-century Russian count. This old-world dish is best reserved for chilly nights, served with a bottle of good red wine.

STEAK & MUSHROOM STROGANOFF

Makes 4 servings

Beef sirloin steak, 1½ pounds (750 g)

Kosher salt and freshly ground pepper

Wide egg noodles, ¾ pound (375 g)

Canola oil, 2 tablespoons plus more as needed

Button or cremini mushrooms, 1 pound (500 g), sliced

Unsalted butter, 3 tablespoons

Shallots, ⅓ cup (2 oz/60 g) minced

Sour cream, 1½ cups (12 oz/375 g), at room temperature

Fresh dill, 1 tablespoon minced, plus more for garnish

Trim the steak of any surface fat. Cut the steak across the grain into slices ¼ inch (6 mm) thick, then cut the slices into 2-inch (5-cm) lengths. Season with salt and pepper.

Bring a large pot of salted water to a boil over high heat. Add the egg noodles and stir occasionally until the water returns to a boil. Cook according to the package directions until al dente.

While the noodles are cooking, brown the steak. In a large frying pan, heat the oil over medium-high heat until it shimmers. Add the steak in batches and cook, stirring frequently, until lightly browned and still quite rare, about 1½ minutes per batch, adding more oil to the pan as needed. Transfer the beef to a plate.

When all the steak is cooked, add the mushrooms and 2 tablespoons of the butter to the frying pan and cook over medium-high heat, stirring frequently, until the mushrooms are lightly browned, about 6 minutes. Add the shallots and cook, stirring occasionally, until they soften, about 2 minutes. Remove from the heat and stir in the steak, sour cream, and the 1 tablespoon dill. Return to medium heat and simmer, stirring constantly, until the sour cream is heated through, about 1 minute. Do not allow to boil. Season with salt and pepper.

When the noodles are ready, drain them and return to the cooking pot. Add the remaining 1 tablespoon butter and toss to coat. Divide the noodles among dinner plates and top each serving with the steak and sauce. Sprinkle with dill and serve.

Change it up You can also make this dish with 1½ pounds (750 g) thin veal cutlets, cut into strips ½ inch (12 mm) wide. Or try leftover steak. You'll need about 2 cups (12 oz/370 g) of steak, cut into bite-sized cubes. Simply add it to the mushroom mixture along with the sour cream and heat through.

Meat loaf rarely gets points for good looks, but it sure can be delicious! Use beef, veal, and pork, a trio that yields an especially flavorful loaf that is also easy to slice. And don't neglect to make gravy from the pan drippings to spoon over the meat loaf and, of course, over a mountain of Buttery Mashed Potatoes (page 158).

CLASSIC MEATLOAF

Makes 6 servings

Canola oil, for the pan

Yellow onion, 1, minced

Dried bread crumbs, ½ cup (2 oz/60 g)

Ketchup (page 215 or purchased), ½ cup (4 oz/125 g) plus 3 tablespoons

Large eggs, 2, beaten

Worcestershire sauce, 2 tablespoons

Kosher salt and freshly ground pepper

Ground beef, 1 pound (500 g)

Ground pork, ½ pound (250 g)

Ground veal, ½ pound (250 g)

Unsalted butter, about 1 tablespoon

All-purpose flour, 2 tablespoons

Beef Stock (page 212) or broth, 2 cups (16 fl oz/500 ml)

Preheat the oven to 350°F (180°C). Lightly oil a small roasting pan.

In a large bowl, combine the onion, bread crumbs, the ½ cup (4 oz/125 g) ketchup, eggs, Worcestershire sauce, 1 teaspoon salt, and ½ teaspoon pepper. Add the meats and mix with your hands just until combined. Transfer the mixture to the prepared pan and shape it into a thick loaf about 9 inches (23 cm) long.

Bake the meatloaf for 45 minutes. Spread the top of the meatloaf with the remaining 3 tablespoons ketchup and bake until an instant-read thermometer inserted in the center registers 165°F (74°C), about 15 minutes longer. Remove from the oven and let stand in the pan for 5 minutes. Using a large, wide spatula, transfer the meatloaf to a platter and tent with aluminum foil to keep warm.

To make the gravy, pour the fat out of the roasting pan. Measure 2 tablespoons fat, adding butter as needed to supplement it, and return the fat to the pan. Heat the roasting pan over medium heat until the butter melts. Whisk in the flour and let bubble for 1 minute. Gradually whisk in the stock and bring to a boil. Reduce the heat to medium-low and simmer, whisking frequently, until a lightly thickened gravy forms, about 5 minutes. Season with salt and pepper. Strain through a sieve into a warmed sauceboat. Slice the meatloaf and serve hot, passing the gravy on the side.

Change it up   Make a double batch of meatloaf so you will have leftovers for sandwiches. Serve the sliced meatloaf on thick bread slices or torpedo rolls with ketchup or grainy mustard and tomato slices.

A hefty corned beef brisket and a bushel of vegetables simmering in a pot on the stovetop signals the St. Patrick's Day feast. But this simple-to-prepare celebratory supper is too good to serve just one day of the year. Plus, you can put any leftovers to delicious use on Reuben Sandwiches (page 33).

CORNED BEEF & CABBAGE

Makes 6-8 servings

Fresh thyme, 3 sprigs

Fresh flat-leaf parsley, 5 sprigs

Corned beef brisket, 1 (about 3½ pounds/ 1.75 kg)

Bay leaves, 2

Black peppercorns, 1 teaspoon

White boiling onions, 12

Carrots, 6, cut into large chunks

Small red-skinned potatoes, 2 pounds (1 kg)

Green cabbage, 1 small head, cut into 6–8 wedges

Heavy cream, 1 cup (8 fl oz/250 ml)

Prepared horseradish, 3 tablespoons

Kosher salt

Tie together the thyme and parsley sprigs with kitchen string. Rinse the brisket, put it in a large Dutch oven, and add water to cover by 1 inch (2.5 cm). Bring to a boil over medium-high heat, skimming off any foam that rises to the surface. Add the herb bundle, bay leaves, and peppercorns, reduce the heat to medium-low, cover, and simmer gently until almost tender, 2½–3 hours.

Add the onions, carrots, unpeeled potatoes, and cabbage wedges to the pot and return the liquid to a simmer. Cook until the vegetables and brisket are fully tender, about 25 minutes.

Meanwhile, to make the horseradish cream, in a bowl, using a whisk or a handheld mixer, beat the cream until soft peaks form. Using the whisk, fold in the horseradish, then season with salt. Cover and refrigerate the horseradish cream until ready to serve.

Using a slotted spoon, transfer the vegetables to a large platter. Transfer the brisket to a cutting board. Slice the meat across the grain and arrange on the platter with the vegetables. Serve hot, passing the horseradish cream on the side.

Change it up Corning your own beef brisket is easy, but it takes some planning. To make the brine, in a large bowl, combine 8 cups water (64 fl oz/2 l), 1½ cups (12 oz/ 370 g) kosher salt, ½ cup (4 oz/125 g) sugar, 3 tablespoons pickling spices, and 3 cloves garlic, crushed. Stir until the salt and sugar are dissolved. Submerge one 4-pound (2-kg) brisket in the mixture, cover, and refrigerate for 5–8 days. When you are ready to cook, remove the brisket from the brine, rinse well under running cold water, and then proceed with the recipe as directed.

Stir-fried rice noodles in a light brown sauce, chow fun is one of the great Chinese comfort foods. Dried Asian rice noodles (the wide ones used for pad Thai) are now available at supermarkets, so you can make this take-out classic at home. Here, the tender ribbons are accented with bits of marinated beef and crisp-tender broccoli.

BEEF & BROCCOLI CHOW FUN

Makes 4 servings

Flank steak, 12 ounces (375 g)

Soy sauce, 1 tablespoon

Chinese rice wine (or dry sherry), 2 tablespoons

Cornstarch, 2 teaspoons

Dark sesame oil, 2 teaspoons

Light or dark brown sugar, ½ teaspoon

Dried wide rice noodles, 7–8 ounces (220–250 g)

Oyster sauce, 2 tablespoons

Black bean sauce and water, 1 tablespoon *each*

Peanut or vegetable oil, 3 tablespoons

Garlic, 2 cloves, minced

Fresh ginger, 2 teaspoon, peeled and minced

Yellow onion, 1 small, cut into thin half-moons

Broccoli, 1 cup (2 oz/60 g) small florets

Scallions, 3, white and green parts, chopped into 1-inch (2.5-cm) pieces

To prepare the flank steak, cut the steak across the grain into slices ¼-inch (6-mm) thick, and then into pieces about 2 inches (5 cm) long. In a medium bowl, whisk the soy sauce, 1 tablespoon of the rice wine, the cornstarch, 1 teaspoon of the sesame oil, and sugar to dissolve the cornstarch. Add the flank steak and toss well. Let stand for about 15 minutes.

Meanwhile, to prepare the rice noodles, in another medium bowl, soak the noodles in enough hot tap water to cover, stirring occasionally, until they are almost tender, about 10 minutes. Drain, rinse under cold running water, drain again, and toss with the remaining 1 teaspoon sesame oil.

To make the sauce, in a small bowl, whisk the oyster sauce, black bean sauce, water, and the remaining 1 tablespoon rice wine together to combine.

Heat a large wok or frying pan over medium-high heat. Add 1 tablespoon of the peanut oil and swirl to coat the bottom and sides of the wok. Add the flank steak and its marinade, laying the slices as flat as possible, and cook until the undersides are browned, about 1 minute. Stir the steak, add the garlic and ginger, and stir-fry just until the steak loses its raw look, about 1 minute. Transfer the mixture to a platter and wipe out the wok with paper towels.

Return the wok to medium-high heat. Add the remaining 2 tablespoons peanut oil to the wok and swirl as before. Add the onion and cook, without stirring, until browned on the edges, about 1 minute. Add the broccoli and scallions and stir-fry until the broccoli is crisp-tender, about 1 minute. Add the rice noodles and steak mixture and stir-fry to until the noodles are hot, about 1 minute. Add the sauce mixture and stir-fry until the noodles are coated, about 30 seconds. Transfer to a platter and serve hot.

Lighten it up

For seafood chow fun, substitute 12 ounces (375 g) peeled and deveined large shrimp, cut in half lengthwise, for the beef. Or omit the broccoli florets and add 3 cups (12 oz/375 g) fresh bean sprouts to the wok with the sauce mixture.

Back in the day, Swiss steak was a supermarket staple. You would pick out a round steak and the butcher would put it through the "Swissing" machine, a contraption that perforated the tough meat to tenderize it. Nowadays, Swiss steaks, sometimes labeled "cube steaks," are harder to find, but this dish makes the search worthwhile.

CHICKEN-FRIED STEAK WITH CREAM GRAVY

Makes 4 servings

Swiss steak or cube steak, 1½ pounds (750 g), no more than ⅛ inch (3 mm) thick

Kosher salt and freshly ground pepper

All-purpose flour, 1¼ cups (6½ oz/200 g) plus 2 tablespoons

Whole milk, 2½ cups (20 fl oz/625 ml)

Large eggs, 2

Canola oil, for frying

Cut the steak into 4 equal pieces. Season the steaks with 1 teaspoon salt and ¼ teaspoon pepper. In a shallow bowl, combine the 1¼ cups (6½ oz/200 g) flour with ½ teaspoon each salt and pepper. In a second shallow bowl, whisk together ½ cup (4 fl oz/125 ml) of the milk and the eggs. One at a time, coat the steak pieces with the flour mixture, shaking off the excess, then dip into the egg mixture, coating evenly and allowing the excess to drip off. Return to the flour mixture to coat evenly, again shaking off the excess. Transfer the coated steak pieces to a plate.

Preheat the oven to 200°F (95°C). Set a wire rack on a rimmed baking sheet and place near the stove. Pour canola oil to a depth of about 1 inch (2.5 cm) into a large, heavy frying pan (preferably cast iron), and heat over medium-high heat until the oil shimmers. Add the steaks and cook until the undersides are golden brown, about 1½ minutes, then turn and cook until the other sides are browned, about 1½ minutes more. Transfer to the rack and keep warm in the oven while making the gravy.

Carefully pour the hot fat from the frying pan into a bowl and set aside. Wipe out the pan with paper towels. In a saucepan, heat the remaining 2 cups (16 fl oz/500 ml) milk over medium heat to just below a boil and remove from the heat. Return 2 tablespoons of the fat to the pan and heat over medium-low heat. Whisk in the remaining 2 tablespoons flour and let bubble gently for 2 minutes. Gradually whisk in the hot milk and bring to a boil over high heat. Reduce the heat to medium-low and simmer, whisking frequently, until lightly thickened, about 3 minutes. Season with salt and pepper and pour into a sauceboat. Serve the steaks at once, passing the gravy on the side.

Change it up   Be sure to make Buttery Mashed Potatoes (page 158), so you can pour a ridiculous amount of the gravy on top. For a spicy version, heat things up with smoky ground chipotle chile. Add ⅛ teaspoon of the ground chile to the steak seasoning and ⅛ teaspoon to the gravy.

You don't need a charcoal grill to make a thick, juicy steak that would make a steakhouse chef green with envy. This thick cut of porterhouse is seared in a hot skillet and finished in the oven, resulting in a savory crust. Top each serving with garlic butter to mingle with the carved meat's juices.

PORTERHOUSE STEAK

Makes 2-3 servings

Porterhouse steak, 1, about 1½ lb (750 g) and 1¼–1½ inches (3–4 cm) thick, patted dry

Olive oil, 1 tablespoon

Unsalted butter, 6 tablespoons (3 oz/90 g), at room temperature

Garlic, 6 cloves, finely chopped

Kosher salt and freshly ground pepper

Rub both sides of the steak with the oil. Let stand at room temperature for 1 hour.

To make the garlic butter, in a small skillet, melt 1 tablespoon of the butter over medium-low heat. Add the garlic and cook, stirring often, until softened but not browned, 2 to 3 minutes. Transfer to a small bowl and let cool. Add the remaining 5 tablespoons (2½ oz/75 g) of butter and stir well. Let stand at room temperature until serving.

Heat a large, ovenproof frying pan over high heat until it is very hot, about 3 minutes. Season the steak on both sides with salt and pepper. Use tongs to place the steak in the pan and reduce the heat to medium-high. Let cook without moving it for 2½ minutes. Turn and cook for 2½ minutes more. Transfer to a rack set over a plate and let stand at room temperature for at least 30 minutes or up to 1 hour.

Preheat the oven to 425°F (220°C). Return the steak to the pan, place in the oven, and cook until an instant-read thermometer inserted into the steak away from the bone registers 130°–135°F (54°–57°C) for medium-rare, about 12 minutes, or to your desired doneness. Transfer to the rack and let rest, uncovered, for 5–8 minutes.

Cut the sirloin away from the bone on one side and the filet section on the other. Cut across the grain into thick slices. Arrange on plates. Serve at once, topping each serving with a dollop of the garlic butter.

When comfort food cravings hit, a heaping plate of spaghetti crowned with plump meatballs is the perfect dish to serve. Make a double batch of the sauce, so you have a container in the freezer, ready at a moment's notice. You can serve the meatballs and sauce atop a bed of roasted zucchini slices for a lighter and gluten-free option.

SPAGHETTI & MEATBALLS

Makes 6 servings

Olive oil, 1 tablespoon

Yellow onion, ½ cup (3 oz/90 g) minced

Garlic, 2 cloves, minced

Coarse fresh bread crumbs, ¾ cup (1½ oz/45 g)

Whole milk, ½ cup (4 fl oz/125 ml)

Egg, 1 large, beaten

Fresh flat-leaf parsley, 2 tablespoons minced

Dried oregano, 1½ teaspoons

Kosher salt, 1½ teaspoons

Freshly ground pepper, ½ teaspoon

Ground beef round, 1 pound (500 g)

Ground pork, ½ pound (250 g)

Ground veal, ½ pound (250 g)

Marinara Sauce (page 215) or purchased, 6 cups (48 oz/1.5 kg)

Spaghetti, 1 pound (500 g)

Freshly grated Parmesan cheese for serving

Preheat the oven to 400°F (200°C). Lightly oil a rimmed baking sheet. In a small frying pan, heat the oil over medium heat. Add the onion and cook, stirring occasionally, until softened, about 4 minutes. Add the garlic and cook until fragrant, about 1 minute more. Transfer to a large bowl and let cool to lukewarm.

Meanwhile, place the bread crumbs in a small bowl. Add the milk and let stand for 5 minutes. Transfer the mixture to a sieve and drain, pressing hard on the bread to extract the excess milk. Add the soaked bread crumbs, egg, parsley, oregano, salt, and pepper to the onion mixture and mix well. Add the ground meats and mix with your hands just until combined. Do not overmix, or the meatballs will be dense.

Using wet hands, shape the mixture into 18 meatballs, and arrange on the prepared baking sheet. Bake until the tops are browned, about 20 minutes, then turn and bake until cooked through, 15 minutes more. Remove from the oven.

In a large saucepan, bring the marinara sauce to a simmer over medium heat. Add the meatballs. Discard any fat on the baking sheet, add ½ cup (4 fl oz/125 ml) boiling water to the baking sheet, and use a wooden spatula to scrape up any browned bits. Pour into the marinara sauce and stir. Simmer until the flavors are blended, about 20 minutes.

Meanwhile, bring a large pot of salted water to a boil over high heat. Add the spaghetti and stir occasionally until the water returns to a boil. Cook according to the package directions until al dente. Drain in a colander. Return the pasta to the pot. Add about half of the sauce to the pasta, without the meatballs, and toss to combine. Divide the pasta among individual pasta bowls, and top each serving with more sauce and an equal number of the meatballs. Serve hot, with the Parmesan.

Change it up For a great baked dish, substitute ziti for the spaghetti and undercook it slightly. Toss the drained pasta with the meatballs and sauce, transfer to a baking dish, and top with 1 cup (4 oz/125 g) freshly grated Parmesan. Bake in a preheated 350°F (180°C) oven until the cheese is browned, about 15 minutes.

Homemade gnocchi is the kind of hands-on dish that seems like it would take a family of gray-haired aunts to make. But these featherlight potato dumplings, tossed with fragrant basil pesto, are remarkably easy to shape. You can make the gnocchi up to 8 hours in advance and refrigerate them until 1 hour before cooking.

POTATO GNOCCHI WITH PESTO

Makes 4-6 servings

Baking potatoes,
1²/₃ pounds (800 g)

Kosher salt

Large eggs, 2, beaten

All-purpose flour, about
1¹/₃ cups (7 oz/215 g), or
as needed

**Basil Pesto (page 215
or purchased),**
½ cup (4½ oz/120 g)

**Freshly grated Parmesan
cheese for serving**

In a large saucepan, combine the unpeeled potatoes with salted water to cover by 1 inch (2.5 cm), cover the pan, and bring to a boil over high heat. Reduce the heat to medium-low and simmer until tender when pierced with a knife, about 30 minutes. Drain and rinse with cold running water until easy to handle. Peel the potatoes and return them to the saucepan. Cook over medium-low heat, shaking the pan often, to evaporate the excess moisture, about 2 minutes.

Press the warm potatoes through a ricer or rub them through a coarse-mesh sieve into a bowl. Stir in the eggs and 2 teaspoons salt. Gradually stir in enough of the flour to make a soft dough, taking care not to add too much. Turn the dough out onto a lightly floured work surface and knead gently a few times until it is smooth, adding just enough flour to prevent sticking. Divide the dough into 4 equal portions.

Lightly flour a rimmed baking sheet. Using floured hands, transfer 1 portion of the dough to a lightly floured work surface. Using your palms, roll the dough to make a rope about ¾ inch (2 cm) in diameter. Cut the rope into 1-inch (2.5-cm) lengths and transfer to the prepared baking sheet. Repeat with the remaining dough.

Bring a large pot of salted water to a boil over high heat. Add half of the gnocchi to the water and simmer until they rise to the surface, then cook 1 minute longer. Using a skimmer, carefully transfer the gnocchi to a warmed serving bowl and cover to keep warm. Repeat with the remaining gnocchi, then scoop out ½ cup (4 fl oz/125 ml) of the cooking water and discard the remainder.

Add the pesto and about ¼ cup (2 fl oz/60 ml) of the reserved cooking water to the gnocchi. Toss gently, adding more water as needed to make a creamy sauce. Serve at once, passing Parmesan on the side.

Change it up Gnocchi will hold up to a variety of different sauces, from brown butter and sage or Marinara Sauce (page 215) to a hearty Bolognese Sauce (page 134).

Luscious, creamy, indulgent—these are all apt words to describe fettuccine Alfredo, one of the great Italian pasta dishes. Invented by a Roman restaurateur, it has only a few ingredients artfully blended (follow the easy instructions carefully) to create its smooth sauce.

FETTUCCINE ALFREDO WITH ROASTED CAULIFLOWER

Makes 4 servings

Cauliflower, 1 head, cut into bite-sized florets about 1½-inches (4-cm) across

Extra-virgin olive oil, 2 tablespoons

Kosher salt and freshly ground pepper

Dried fettuccine, 1 pound (16 oz/500 g)

Heavy cream, 1 cup (8 fl oz/250 ml)

Unsalted butter, ½ cup (4 oz/125 g), cut into tablespoons, at room temperature

Parmesan cheese, 2 cups (8 oz/250 g) freshly grated

Flat-leaf parsley, 2 tablespoons freshly chopped

Preheat the oven to 425°F (220°C). Toss the cauliflower with the oil on a rimmed baking sheet and season with salt and pepper. Roast, flipping the cauliflower after 15 minutes, until tender and lightly browned, about 30 minutes.

Meanwhile, bring a large pot of salted water to a boil over high heat. Add the fettuccine and stir occasionally until the water returns to a boil. Cook according to the package directions until it is al dente.

While the pasta is cooking, in a small saucepan, bring the cream to a simmer over medium heat. Set the hot cream aside.

Drain the fettuccine well and return it to its warm cooking pot. Add the hot cream and butter and toss with two wooden spatulas or spoons until the butter is almost completely melted. In two or three additions, sprinkle in the Parmesan and toss well until it is melted. Season with salt and pepper. Add the roasted cauliflower and parsley and toss again. Serve at once.

Lighten it up   To add protein to the dish, substitute chunks of cooked chicken, shrimp, or seafood, lightly sautéed in a little butter just until warmed. Broccoli is a fine substitute for the cauliflower. You can also add other cubed, roasted vegetables, such as carrots, sweet potatoes, and Brussels sprouts. Use gluten-free pasta, if you wish.

By nature, risotto is a comforting dish, with a soft texture and loose consistency. Almost constant stirring releases the starch from the rice grains to give the cooking liquid its unique creaminess. Here, a basic risotto mixture is finished with an earthy mix of fresh portobello, dried porcini mushrooms, and nutty Parmesan.

MUSHROOM RISOTTO

Makes 4 servings

Dried porcini mushrooms, 1 ounce (30 g)

Boiling water, 1 cup (8 fl oz/250 ml)

Extra-virgin olive oil, 2 tablespoons

Portobello mushrooms, 1 pound (500 g), stems and caps cut into ½-inch (12-mm) dice

Shallots, 3 tablespoons finely chopped

Fresh thyme, 1 teaspoon finely chopped

Chicken Stock (page 212) or broth, 4 cups (32 fl oz/1 l)

Unsalted butter, 2 tablespoons

Yellow onion, 1, finely chopped

Garlic, 1 clove, minced

Risotto rice, such as Arborio, 1½ cups (10 oz/330 g)

Dry white wine, ½ cup (4 fl oz/125 ml)

Parmesan cheese, ½ cup (2 oz/60 g) freshly grated, plus more for serving

Kosher salt and freshly ground pepper

In a small bowl, cover the porcini with the boiling water. Let stand until the porcini is softened, 20–30 minutes. Lift out the porcini, coarsely chop it, and transfer to another small bowl. Strain the soaking liquid through a fine wire mesh strainer into the porcini, leaving any grit in the bottom of the soaking bowl.

In a large frying pan, heat the oil over medium-high heat. Add the portobello and cook, stirring occasionally, until lightly browned, about 3 minutes. Add the shallots and cook, stirring occasionally, until softened, about 2 minutes. Add the porcini and their liquid and bring to a boil. Cook until the liquid reduces by half, about 3 minutes. Stir in the thyme. Set aside.

Meanwhile, in a medium saucepan, bring the stock and 2 cups (16 fl oz/500 ml) water to a simmer over high heat. Reduce the heat to low to keep the liquid at a low simmer.

Melt the butter in a flameproof casserole over medium heat. Add the onion and garlic and cook, stirring occasionally, until softened. Add the rice and cook, stirring frequently, until it is well-coated with the butter but not browned, about 2 minutes. Add the wine and boil until reduced to 2 tablespoons. Ladle in ¾ cup (6 fl oz/180 ml) of the hot stock mixture and reduce the heat to medium-low so it maintains a steady simmer. Stir almost constantly until the rice has absorbed about two-thirds of the stock mixture. Repeat, adding the hot stock mixture in ¾ cup (6 fl oz/180 ml) increments and stirring until it is completely absorbed, until the rice is barely tender, 20–25 minutes. (If the hot stock mixture is used before the rice is tender, use simmering water.) Add the Parmesan and stir until it melts. Season the risotto with salt and pepper.

Stir about half of the mushroom mixture into the risotto. Stir in a final addition of the stock—it should have a loose, but not soupy, consistency. Divide among four soup bowls, and top each with an equal amount of the remaining mushroom mixture. Serve hot, with additional Parmesan passed on the side.

Change it up   For a heartier risotto, add 8 ounces (250 g) of separately cooked, crumbled Italian sausage (sweet or hot, pork or poultry) to the cooked mushroom mixture.

A simple tomato sauce is the perfect backdrop for this classic pie oozing with melted mozzarella and studded with savory pork sausage and sliced mushrooms. One secret to great pizza is great dough, and the key to great dough is a slow rise. For the best results, make the dough at least 9 or 10 hours before baking.

NEW YORK-STYLE SAUSAGE & MUSHROOM PIZZA

Makes two 12-inch (30-cm) pizzas

Pizza Dough (page 216)

Canned crushed plum tomatoes, 1 cup (7 oz/220 g)

Extra-virgin olive oil, 2 tablespoons

Dried oregano, 1 teaspoon

Cremini or button mushrooms, ½ pound (250 g), sliced

Kosher salt and freshly ground pepper

Sweet or hot Italian pork sausages, ½ pound (250 g), casings removed

All-purpose or bread flour and cornmeal for dusting

Fresh mozzarella cheese, 1 pound (500 g), thinly sliced

Parmesan cheese, 4 tablespoons (1 oz/30 g) freshly grated

The night before serving, prepare the pizza dough and refrigerate. Remove the dough from the refrigerator 1—2 hours before forming the pizzas. Position a rack in the lower third of the oven. Place a large pizza stone on the rack, and preheat the oven to 450°F (230°C), allowing at least 30 minutes for the oven to preheat fully.

To make the pizza sauce, in a bowl, mix together the tomatoes, 1 tablespoon of the oil, and the oregano. Set aside.

To prepare the toppings, in a large frying pan, heat the remaining 1 tablespoon oil over medium-high heat. Add the mushrooms and cook, stirring, until they give off their juices and are browned, about 8 minutes. Transfer to a bowl and season with salt and pepper. Add the sausages to the pan and cook over medium-high heat, stirring and breaking them up with a wooden spoon, until no longer pink, about 10 minutes. Transfer to the bowl with the mushrooms. Set aside.

Divide the dough in half and shape each half into a taut ball. Place 1 ball on a lightly floured work surface. Return the other dough ball to its bowl and cover. Roll, pat, and stretch the dough into a round about 12 inches (30 cm) in diameter.

Generously dust a pizza peel with flour. Transfer the dough to the peel and reshape into a round as needed. Spread with half of the sauce, leaving a ¾-inch (2-cm) border uncovered. Top with half of the mozzarella, then half of the mushroom mixture.

Slide the pizza off the peel onto the hot stone. Bake until the crust is golden brown, about 12 minutes. While the first pizza is baking, repeat with the remaining dough, tomato sauce, mozzarella, and mushroom mixture, so the second pizza is ready to bake when the first one comes out of the oven. Using a wide spatula or a rimless baking sheet, remove the baked pizza from the oven and transfer to a cutting board. Sprinkle with half of the Parmesan cheese. Slide the second pizza onto the hot stone and bake for about 12 minutes. Cut and serve the first pizza. When the second pizza is done, top with the remaining Parmesan cheese, cut, and serve.

Tender eggplant under a cloak of garlicky tomato sauce and melted cheese: who doesn't love eggplant Parmesan? Even picky eaters who think they don't like eggplant like this dish. In this simplified version, the breaded eggplant is "oven-fried" instead of pan-fried, which means less oil and less mess, but no less flavor.

EGGPLANT PARMESAN

Makes 4-6 servings

Eggplants, 2 small (about ¾ pound/375 g each)

Kosher salt

Extra-virgin olive oil, ¼ cup (2 fl oz/60 ml)

Large eggs, 3

Whole milk, 2 tablespoons

All-purpose flour, 1 cup (5 oz/155 g)

Dried oregano, 1 teaspoon

Freshly ground pepper, ½ teaspoon

Fine dried bread crumbs, 2 cups (8 oz/150 g)

Parmesan cheese, ¾ cup (3 oz/90 g) freshly grated

Marinara Sauce (page 215) or purchased, 3 cups (24 oz/750 g)

Fresh mozzarella cheese, 1 pound (500 g), sliced

Thinly slice the eggplants crosswise diagonally. Place a large wire rack on a rimmed baking sheet. Sprinkle both sides of each eggplant slice with salt. Set the slices on the rack and let stand for about 30 minutes. Wipe the slices with paper towels to blot the moisture and remove excess salt.

Preheat the oven to 425°F (220°C). Drizzle a large rimmed baking sheet with the oil. In a shallow bowl, whisk together the eggs and milk. In a second shallow bowl, stir together the flour, oregano, and pepper. In a third shallow bowl, combine the bread crumbs and ¼ cup (1 oz/30 g) of the Parmesan. One at a time, coat the eggplant slices with the flour mixture, shaking off the excess, then dip into the egg mixture, coating evenly and allowing the excess to drip off. Finally, dip into the bread crumb mixture, patting gently to help it adhere. Transfer to the prepared baking sheet. Bake for 15 minutes. Turn the eggplant slices over and continue to bake until golden brown, about 15 minutes more. Let cool until easy to handle, 5–10 minutes. Leave the oven on.

Lightly oil a 9-by-13-inch (23-by-33-cm) baking dish. Spread 1 cup (8 oz/250 g) of the marinara sauce in the bottom of the prepared dish. Layer half of the eggplant slices, overlapping them to fit, on top of the sauce, then spoon 1 cup (8 oz/250 g) of the sauce evenly over the slices.

Top with half of the mozzarella, and sprinkle with ¼ cup (1 oz/30 g) of the Parmesan. Repeat with the remaining eggplant, marinara sauce, mozzarella, and Parmesan. Bake until the cheese is melted and the sauce is bubbling, about 30 minutes. Let stand for 10 minutes, then serve hot.

Change it up For an eggplant Parmesan panini, brush 2 slices pain au levain or other rustic bread on both sides with olive oil. On 1 bread slice, layer mozzarella slices, oven-fried eggplant slices, marinara sauce, and more mozzarella slices, in that order. Top with a second bread slice. Using a panini grill, toast the sandwich until the bread is browned and the cheese is melted.

Layers of tender pasta, slow-cooked meat sauce, and creamy béchamel—this satisfying lasagna is ideal for feeding a crowd, and is simply one of the most perfect comfort foods. Busy hosts will appreciate that it can be prepared in advance. Assemble it, then cover and refrigerate for up to 12 hours, before baking.

LASAGNA BOLOGNESE

Makes 8 servings

Olive oil, 1 tablespoon

Pancetta, ¼ pound (125 g), diced

Yellow onions, 2 small

Carrot and celery, 1 each, finely chopped

Garlic, 2 cloves, minced

Ground beef, pork, and veal, 1 pound (500 g) each

Dry white wine, 1 cup (8 fl oz/250 ml)

Plum tomatoes, 1 can (28 ounces/875 g)

Dried basil and oregano, 1 teaspoon each

Kosher salt and freshly ground pepper

Bay leaves, 3

Heavy cream, ½ cup (4 fl oz/125 ml)

Whole milk, 4 cups (32 fl oz/1 l)

Unsalted butter, ½ cup (4 oz/125 g) plus 1 tablespoon, diced

All-purpose flour, ½ cup (2½ oz/75 g)

Plain or fresh spinach pasta sheets, ¾ pound (375 g)

Parmesan cheese, 1 cup (4 oz/125 g) freshly grated

To make the Bolognese sauce, in a large saucepan, heat the oil over medium heat. Add the pancetta and cook, stirring often, until lightly browned, about 8 minutes. Finely chop 1 onion and add to the pan along with the carrot and celery. Cover and cook, stirring occasionally, until the vegetables soften, about 5 minutes. Stir in the garlic and cook until fragrant, about 1 minute. Add the ground meats and increase the heat to medium-high. Cook, stirring and breaking them up with a wooden spoon, until no longer pink, about 10 minutes. Add the wine and cook until it has almost evaporated, about 5 minutes. Crush the tomatoes with your fingers. Stir in the tomatoes and their juice, basil, oregano, 2 teaspoons salt, 1 teaspoon pepper, and 2 of the bay leaves and bring to a boil. Reduce the heat to low and simmer uncovered, stirring occasionally, until the tomatoes break down and a thick, meaty sauce forms, adding a little water if the sauce thickens too much, about 1¾ hours. Add the cream and simmer for 15 minutes more. Discard the bay leaves.

To make the béchamel, thickly slice the remaining onion and place in a saucepan. Add the milk and the remaining bay leaf and bring slowly to a simmer over medium heat. Cover, remove from the heat, and let stand 10 minutes. Discard the onion and bay leaf. In another saucepan, melt the ½ cup (4 oz/125 g) butter over medium heat. Whisk in the flour. Reduce the heat to medium-low and let bubble for 1 minute. Gradually whisk in the warm milk, raise the heat to medium, and bring to a gentle boil, whisking frequently. Reduce the heat to medium-low and simmer, whisking frequently, until smooth and lightly thickened, about 5 minutes. Season with salt and pepper.

Meanwhile, preheat the oven to 350°F (180°C). Butter a 10-by-15-inch (25-by-38-cm) baking dish. To assemble, cut the pasta sheets into 15-inch (38-cm) lengths. Spread ½ cup (4 oz/125 g) of béchamel in the bottom of the baking dish. Top with a layer of pasta, one-third of the Bolognese, one-fourth of the béchamel, and ¼ cup (1 oz/30 g) of the Parmesan. Repeat two more times with layers of pasta, Bolognese, bechamel, and Parmesan. Finish with a final layer of pasta, the remaining béchamel and Parmesan, and the 1 tablespoon diced butter. Bake, uncovered, until the béchamel is lightly browned and the sauce is bubbling, about 30 minutes. Let stand for 10 minutes, then cut into squares and serve hot.

This version is more generously proportioned than most, with enough flavorful Italian sausage, roasted eggplant, and tangy tomato sauce, that the dish isn't completely focused around pasta. Round out this satisfying meal with a big green salad and your favorite wine.

BAKED ZITI WITH SAUSAGE

Makes 6 servings

Olive oil, 4 tablespoons (2 fl oz/60 ml), plus more for the baking dish

Eggplants, 2 small (about ¾ pound/375 g each)

Sweet or hot Italian pork sausages, 1 pound (500 g), casings removed

Yellow onion, 1, chopped

Garlic, 2 cloves, minced

Hearty red wine, ½ cup (4 fl oz/125 ml)

Crushed plum tomatoes, 1 can (28 ounces/875 g)

Dried oregano, 2 teaspoons

Red pepper flakes, ½ teaspoon, plus more as needed

Kalamata olives, ½ cup (5 oz/155 g) pitted and coarsely chopped

Kosher salt

Ziti or other tubular pasta, 1 pound (500 g)

Ricotta cheese, 2 cups (16 oz/500 g)

Parmesan cheese, ½ cup (2 oz/60 g) freshly grated

Preheat the oven to 400°F (200°C). Lightly oil a 3-quart (3-l) baking dish or 6 individual baking dishes. Cut the eggplants into bite-sized cubes. Spread the cubes on a large rimmed baking sheet. Drizzle with 3 tablespoons of the oil and toss to coat. Roast, stirring occasionally, until tender and lightly browned, about 30 minutes.

Meanwhile, in a large, heavy saucepan, heat the remaining 1 tablespoon oil over medium-high heat. Add the sausages and cook, stirring and breaking them up with a wooden spoon, until no longer pink, about 10 minutes. Using a slotted spoon, transfer to a plate. Pour off all but 2 tablespoons of the fat in the pan.

Add the onion to the pan and cook over medium heat, stirring, until tender, about 5 minutes. Stir in the garlic and cook until fragrant, about 1 minute. Add the wine, stir to loosen any browned bits on the pan bottom, and bring to a boil. Stir in the tomatoes, oregano, and red pepper flakes and bring to a boil. Return the sausage to the pan and stir in the eggplant. Reduce the heat to medium-low and simmer until thickened, about 20 minutes. Stir in the olives and remove from the heat.

Meanwhile, bring a large pot of salted water to a boil over high heat. Add the ziti and stir occasionally until the water returns to a boil. Cook according to the package directions until not quite al dente. (The ziti should not be cooked all the way through, as it will finish cooking in the oven.) Drain well. Add the ziti to the sauce along with the ricotta, and stir until combined. Season with salt, taste, and adjust the seasoning with red pepper flakes. Spread the pasta mixture in the prepared baking dish(es) and sprinkle evenly with the Parmesan. Bake until the sauce is bubbling and the Parmesan is golden, about 20 minutes. Let stand for 5 minutes, then serve.

Lighten it up For a meatless adaptation of this dish, substitute 1¼ pounds (625 g) cremini mushrooms, quartered, for the sausage, and finely chopped fresh rosemary for the oregano. Sauté the mushrooms in the olive oil (you may need more oil) over medium-high heat until tender, about 8 minutes.

Pasta recipes are high on the list of soul-satisfying suppers, with this old-world classic among the most popular of the clan: briny fresh clams in a garlicky wine sauce and a generous dusting of fresh parsley. Clams are low in calories and high in protein, making this dish even more satisfying.

LINGUINE WITH CLAMS

Makes 4 servings

Littleneck clams, 3 dozen (about 3 pounds/1.5 kg)

Kosher salt

Linguine, 1 pound (500 g)

Extra-virgin olive oil, ¼ cup (2 fl oz/60 ml)

Garlic, 3 cloves, minced

Red pepper flakes, ¼ teaspoon, or to taste

Dry white wine, ½ cup (4 fl oz/125 ml)

Unsalted butter, 2 tablespoons

Fresh flat-leaf parsley, 3 tablespoons finely chopped

Scrub the clams well under cold running water. Place in a large bowl, add salted cold water to cover, and let stand for 1 hour. Drain the clams and rinse well. Meanwhile, bring a large pot of salted water to a boil over high heat. Add the linguine and stir occasionally until the water returns to a boil. Cook according to the package directions until al dente.

While the linguine is cooking, in a large saucepan over medium heat, add the olive oil, garlic, and red pepper flakes and cook until the garlic softens and is fragrant but not browned, about 3 minutes. Add the clams and wine and cover. Increase the heat to high and cook, shaking the pan occasionally by its handle, until the clams have opened, about 4 minutes. Remove from the heat and discard any unopened clams.

Add the butter and swirl the saucepan to melt the butter into the cooking liquid.

Drain the linguine and return it to its cooking pot. Pour the clams and sauce over the linguine and mix gently. Transfer to a serving platter or individual pasta bowls, dividing the clams evenly. Sprinkle with the parsley and serve at once.

Lighten it up If you can't stand the idea of serving pasta without tomatoes, in a frying pan, sauté 2 cups (12 oz/375 g) whole grape or cherry tomatoes in 2 tablespoons olive oil over high heat until they are hot and begin to wilt, 3—4 minutes. Add them to the clams and their sauce along with the pasta.

Almost everybody likes crunchy fish fillets with a heap of crisp fries, and you can successfully make this British dish at home if you time the steps carefully. These fries—chips to the British—are "oven-fried" to ease the cook's workload and cut out excess fat. Keep the meal balanced and in-theme with a side of steamed peas.

FISH & CHIPS

Makes 4 servings

TARTAR SAUCE

Mayonnaise (page 216 or purchased), 1 cup (8 fl oz/250 ml)

Sweet pickle relish, 2 tablespoons

Nonpareil capers, 1 tablespoon, rinsed

Fresh flat-leaf parsley, 1 tablespoon minced

Cake flour, 1 cup (4 oz/125 g)

Baking powder, 1½ teaspoons

Kosher salt

Lager beer, ½ cup (4 fl oz/125 ml), or as needed

Large egg, 1, beaten

Canola oil, 5 tablespoons (3 fl oz/80 ml) plus more for frying

Baking potatoes, 4 large

Skinless haddock or cod fillet, 1¼ pounds (625 g), cut into 4 pieces

Malt vinegar and lemon wedges for serving

To make the tartar sauce, in a bowl, mix together the mayonnaise, relish, capers, and parsley. Cover and refrigerate for at least 1 hour to allow the flavors to blend.

To make the batter, in a bowl, whisk together the flour, baking powder, and ½ teaspoon salt. Add the ½ cup (4 fl oz/125 ml) beer, the egg, and 2 tablespoons of the oil and whisk just until the ingredients are combined (it should be slightly lumpy). The mixture should have the consistency of pancake batter; add more beer if needed.

Let stand at room temperature for about 1 hour while you prepare the potatoes.

To make the chips, position racks in the center and upper third of the oven and preheat to 400°F (200°C). Cut each unpeeled potato in half lengthwise, then cut the halves lengthwise into wedges about ½ inch (12 mm) thick. Arrange the wedges in a single layer on 2 rimmed baking sheets, drizzle with the remaining 3 tablespoons oil, and toss to coat. Place 1 sheet on each oven rack and bake for 20 minutes. Turn the potato wedges, then switch the pans between the racks, rotate the pans 180 degrees, and continue to bake until tender and golden brown, about 25 minutes more.

Just before the chips are finished baking, set a large wire rack on another rimmed baking sheet and place near the stove. Pour oil into a large saucepan to a depth of 3 inches (7.5 cm) and heat over high heat to 350°F (180°C) on a deep-frying thermometer. Remove the chips from the oven. Reduce the oven temperature to 200°F (95°C). Combine the chips on a single baking sheet, season with salt, and return to the oven to keep warm.

In batches to avoid crowding, dip the fish pieces in the batter, letting the excess drip back into the bowl, and add to the hot oil. Deep-fry until golden brown, 3–4 minutes. Transfer to the rack and keep warm in the oven while frying the remaining fish. Serve the fish and chips hot, passing the tartar sauce, vinegar, and lemon wedges.

Change it up For an amazing fried fish sandwich, serve the fried fish and tartar sauce on a soft roll, such as a torpedo roll. Add some shredded lettuce and sliced tomatoes, if you like, and serve the chips on the side.

These tasty tacos, filled with grilled fish and served with a tangy-sweet mango salsa, will have you dreaming of sunny days at the beach, without compromising your waistline. The oil in the marinade coupled with oiling the cooking grate will help prevent the relatively delicate snapper fillets from sticking to the grill grates.

FISH TACOS

Makes 4 servings

Mango, 1

Red onion, 2 tablespoons minced

Fresh cilantro, 3 tablespoons minced

Serrano chile, 1, seeds and ribs removed, minced

Fresh lime juice, 5 tablespoons (3 fl oz/ 80 ml)

Kosher salt

Finely grated lime zest, from 1 lime

Extra-virgin olive oil, 2 tablespoons

Chili powder, 1 teaspoon

Garlic, 1 clove, minced

Skinless red snapper fillets, 1 pound (500 g)

Canola oil for grilling

Corn tortillas, 8

To make the salsa, peel, pit, and dice the mango. In a small bowl, stir together the diced mango, onion, 2 tablespoons cilantro, chile, 3 tablespoons lime juice, and season with salt. Cover the salsa and let stand while preparing the snapper.

Prepare a grill for direct-heat cooking over medium heat. Meanwhile, in a shallow ceramic or glass bowl, whisk together the remaining 2 tablespoons lime juice, the lime zest, olive oil, the remaining 1 tablespoon cilantro, chili powder, and garlic. Add the snapper and turn to coat. Let stand while the grill is heating, no longer than 30 minutes.

Lightly oil the cooking grate. Remove the snapper from the marinade, season it with salt, and place on the grill. (You can use a perforated grill grid if you have one.) Cover and cook until opaque when flaked in the thickest part, about 5 minutes.

(No need to turn the snapper.) Transfer to a cutting board. Do not worry if the snapper pieces fall apart when you remove them from the grill. Tent with aluminum foil to keep warm and let stand for 3 minutes.

Meanwhile, place the tortillas on the grill and cook, turning once, until heated through, about 1 minute total. Wrap in a cloth napkin or kitchen towel to keep warm.

Flake the fish into bite-sized pieces and transfer to a serving plate. Serve at once with the salsa and tortillas, allowing diners to fill their own tacos.

Change it up Fish tacos can be served with slaw instead of salsa: Mix together 4 cups (12 oz/360 g) finely shredded green cabbage; 1 green onion, white and green parts, minced; 1/3 cup (2¾ oz/80 ml) Mayonnaise (page 216 or purchased); 2 tablespoons fresh lime juice; and 2 tablespoons minced fresh cilantro. Season with salt and pepper, and let stand for about 30 minutes before serving.

Shrimp and grits is the kind of old-time Southern comfort that comes in a bowl, and not in a glass. To ensure that not a drop of the delectable sauce is wasted, the plump, pink shrimp are served over soft, cheese-flavored grits. If you like it spicier, pass a bottle of hot sauce at the table.

SHRIMP & GRITS

Makes 4 servings

Vegetable oil, 1 tablespoon

Bacon, 3 strips

Large shrimp, 1½ pounds (750 g), peeled and deveined

All-purpose flour, ¼ cup (1½ oz/45 g)

Red bell pepper, ½ cup (4 oz/125 g) diced

Scallions, 4, white and green parts, chopped

Garlic, 2 cloves, minced

Chicken Stock (page 212) or broth, 1¼ cups (10 fl oz/310 ml)

Heavy cream, ⅓ cup (3 fl oz/80 ml)

Worcestershire sauce, 1 teaspoon

Red pepper sauce, ½ teaspoon

Kosher salt and freshly ground pepper

Creamy Grits (page 213)

Fresh flat-leaf parsley, 1 tablespoon minced

Lemon wedges for serving

In a large frying pan, cook the bacon in the oil over medium heat, turning occasionally, until crisp and browned, about 8 minutes. Transfer the bacon to paper towels to drain and cool. Pour the fat into a small heatproof bowl.

Return 1 tablespoon of the oil to the skillet and heat over medium heat. In a medium bowl, toss the shrimp with the flour, shaking off the flour. Add the shrimp to the skillet and cook, stirring occasionally, just until they turn opaque on the outside, 2—3 minutes. Transfer to a plate.

Add the remaining reserved fat to skillet and heat over medium heat. Add the bell pepper and cook, stirring occasionally, until softened, about 3 minutes. Stir in the scallions and garlic and cook until fragrant, about 1 minute. Add the stock, cream, Worcestershire, and red pepper sauce and bring to a simmer. Reduce the heat to low and simmer gently to blend the flavors, about 5 minutes. Add the shrimp, increase the heat to medium, and return to the simmer. Cook, stirring often, just until the sauce thickens lightly and the shrimp is opaque throughout, about 1 minute. Season with salt and pepper.

To serve, coarsely chop the bacon. Divide the grits evenly among four shallow soup bowls, and top with equal amounts of the shrimp. Sprinkle with the bacon and parsley and serve at once with lemon wedges.

Change it up

Stone-ground grits are not readily available outside of the South. If you use processed old-fashioned or quick grits, follow the instructions on the package, using the broth mixture as the liquid. Or, use stone-ground polenta, which is actually corn grits (coarsely cracked dried corn kernels) from a yellow variety of corn.

Sautéed jumbo shrimp in a buttery, white wine sauce—this dish is delicious served over pasta, rice, Creamy Grits (page 213), or even just a bed of sautéed spinach. The addition of a tablespoon of briny capers and a few pinches of red pepper flakes really elevate the flavors in this dish.

GARLICKY SHRIMP SCAMPI

Makes 4 servings

Jumbo or extra-large shrimp, 1½ pounds (750 g)

All-purpose flour, ½ cup (2½ oz/75 g)

Kosher salt and freshly ground pepper

Olive oil, 2 tablespoons, plus more as needed

Unsalted butter, 12 tablespoons (6 oz/185 g)

Garlic, 3 cloves, minced

Dry white wine, ¼ cup (2 fl oz/60 ml)

Finely grated lemon zest, from 1 lemon

Fresh lemon juice, 2 tablespoons

Fresh flat-leaf parsley, 2 tablespoons finely chopped

Lemon wedges for serving

Peel and devein the shrimp, leaving the tail segment intact. In a shallow bowl, stir together the flour, ½ teaspoon salt, and ¼ teaspoon pepper.

In a large, nonreactive frying pan, heat the oil over medium-high heat. Toss half of the shrimp in the flour mixture to coat evenly, shaking off the excess. Add to the hot oil and cook, turning occasionally, until opaque throughout when pierced with the tip of a knife, about 3 minutes. Transfer to a plate and tent with aluminum foil to keep warm. Repeat with the remaining shrimp, adding more oil as needed.

Reduce the heat to medium-low. Heat 2 tablespoons of the butter and the garlic together in the pan, stirring frequently, until the garlic softens and is fragrant but not browned, about 2 minutes. Add the wine and the lemon zest and juice and bring to a boil over high heat. Cook until reduced by half, about 1 minute. Reduce the heat to very low. One tablespoon at a time, whisk in the remaining 10 tablespoons (5 oz/155 g) butter, letting each addition soften into a creamy emulsion before adding more.

Return the shrimp to the sauce and mix gently to coat well. Remove from the heat and season the sauce with salt and pepper. Transfer to a warmed serving dish and sprinkle with the parsley. Serve at once, passing the lemon wedges on the side.

Change it up Scallops are good with this sauce, too. Small bay scallops will cook in about the same amount of time as the shrimp. If you opt for large sea scallops, sear them in an ovenproof frying pan over high heat for about 1 minute on each side, then slip the browned scallops, still in the pan, into a preheated 400°F (200°C) oven and cook until barely opaque throughout, about 4 minutes. Transfer to a plate, cover to keep warm, and proceed with the recipe to make the sauce.

•SIDES•

Although a grilled steak or cheeseburger and onion rings makes a perfect combination, these crunchy rings can be replaced with vegetables. Try broccoli or cauliflower florets, button mushrooms, or thawed frozen artichoke hearts. Finish with salt and a squeeze of fresh lemon juice, and serve with fried or grilled fish.

BEER-BATTERED ONION RINGS

Makes 4-6 servings

Cake flour, 1 cup (4 oz/125 g)

Large egg, 1

Fine sea salt

Cayenne pepper, ¼ teaspoon

Lager beer, ¾ cup (6 fl oz/180 ml)

Vidalia or yellow onions, 2 large (about 1 pound/500 g total weight)

Canola oil for deep-frying

Ketchup (page 215 or purchased) for serving (optional)

In a bowl, whisk together the flour, egg, ½ teaspoon salt, and the cayenne pepper until blended. Add the beer and whisk just until combined. Do not worry if the batter has a scattering of lumps. Let stand for 30 minutes.

Meanwhile, cut the onions into thick rounds, and separate the rounds into rings.

Pour oil to a depth of at least 3 inches (7.5 cm) into a large, heavy saucepan and heat over high heat to 350°F (180°C) on a deep-frying thermometer. Preheat the oven to 200°F (95°C). Set a large wire rack on a rimmed baking sheet and place near the stove.

In batches to avoid crowding, dip the onion rings into the batter to coat, letting the excess batter drip back into the bowl, and carefully add to the hot oil. Deep-fry until golden brown, about 3 minutes. Using a wire skimmer, transfer to the rack and keep warm in the oven while you fry the remaining onion rings.

Transfer the onion rings to a serving platter and sprinkle with salt. Serve at once with ketchup, if desired.

Old-time Italian American restaurants invariably include cheese-laden garlic bread on their menus. And their regular diners invariably order it, enjoying it alongside a big plate of spaghetti and meatballs. This version is dressed up with fresh herbs and Gruyère cheese for a more contemporary take on that much-loved classic.

GARLIC CHEESE BREAD

Makes 6-8 servings

Unsalted butter,
6 tablespoons (3 oz/90 g),
at room temperature

Garlic, 3 cloves, minced

Parmesan cheese,
3 tablespoons freshly
grated

Fresh basil, 1 tablespoon
minced

Fresh chives,
1 tablespoon minced

Kosher salt, ¼ teaspoon

Italian bread, 1 loaf, split

Gruyère cheese, ¼ cup
(1 oz/30 g) shredded

Fresh flat-leaf parsley,
1½ tablespoons minced

Preheat the oven to 450°F (230°C). Using a rubber spatula, in a small bowl, mash together the butter, garlic, Parmesan, basil, chives, and salt until well blended. Spread the mixture onto the cut sides of the bread, dividing it evenly, then sprinkle evenly with the Gruyère. Place the bread halves, cut sides up, on a rimmed baking sheet.

Bake until the edges of the bread are toasted and the cheese is melted and lightly golden brown, about 10 minutes. Sprinkle evenly with the parsley, cut crosswise into slices, and serve hot.

Change it up Roasted garlic has a sweet, mellow flavor and makes superb garlic bread. Slice a head of garlic in half crosswise, drizzle the halves with olive oil, wrap them in aluminum foil, and place in a small, shallow pan. Bake in a preheated 400°F (200°C) oven until the cloves are soft and creamy, about 35 minutes. Squeeze the cloves from their papery sheaths into the butter mixture in place of the raw garlic.

When you want potatoes you can sink your teeth into, make a batch of these hefty steak fries. To ensure a perfectly crisp exterior and a light and fluffy interior, you need to soak, dry, and double fry the potatoes. To really take it over the top, serve them with homemade ketchup (page 215).

THICK STEAK FRIES

Makes 4 servings

Baking potatoes, 4 large
Canola oil for deep-frying
Sea salt

At least 3½ hours before serving, cut each potato in half lengthwise. Cut each half into wedges about ½ inch (12 mm) thick. Place the wedges in a large bowl and add ice water to cover. Let stand for at least 30 minutes or up to 1 hour. Drain the potatoes well. In batches, spin them dry in a salad spinner, then spread them on kitchen towels, wrap them up, and let stand for 30 minutes more to absorb any remaining moisture.

Pour oil to a depth of at least 3 inches (7.5 cm) into a large, heavy saucepan and heat over high heat to 315°F (158°C) on a deep-frying thermometer. Set a large wire rack on a rimmed baking sheet and place near the stove.

In batches to avoid crowding, add the potatoes to the hot oil and deep-fry, stirring them occasionally with a wooden spoon to separate them, until they turn pale gold and are almost floppy, about 4 minutes. The potatoes should not be browned at this point, though they can be a little browned at the edges. Using a wire skimmer, transfer the potatoes to the rack to drain. Repeat with the remaining potatoes, allowing the oil to return to 315°F (158°C) before adding the next batch. Remove the saucepan with the oil from the heat and set aside. Let the potatoes stand until completely cooled, at least 2 hours or up to 4 hours.

When ready to serve, preheat the oven to 200°F (95°C). Reheat the oil in the saucepan over high heat to 350°F (180°C). Transfer the potatoes to another baking sheet (no need to outfit this one with a rack), so the first baking sheet with its rack is free to hold the fully cooked fries. In batches to avoid crowding, add the potatoes to the hot oil and deep-fry until crisp and golden brown, 2–3 minutes. Transfer to the rack and keep warm in the oven while you fry the remaining potatoes. Transfer to a serving platter and sprinkle with salt. Serve at once.

Change it up   Ketchup is the classic accompaniment for fries in the U.S., but the Belgians love mayonnaise with their fries. For a decadent treat, stir minced fresh herbs (rosemary and thyme are especially good), grated lemon zest, or minced garlic into Mayonnaise (page 216).

Crispy, golden-brown potatoes doused in chile sauce and sprinkled with cheese, sour cream, and green onions—this hearty dish, brimming in flavor, will keep you satisfied for many hours.

PAPAS FRITAS WITH SANTA FE-STYLE CHILE SAUCE

Makes 6 servings

Medium red potatoes, 4½ lb (2.25 kg), scrubbed but unpeeled

Kosher salt and freshly ground pepper

Melted butter, ½ cup (4 fl oz/125 ml) or canola oil

Sweet paprika, 2 teaspoons

Green Chile Sauce (page 213), about 2 cups (16 fl oz/500 ml)

Monterey jack cheese, 1½ cups (6 oz/185 g) shredded

Sour cream, ⅔ cup (5½ oz/170 g), at room temperature

Green onions, 4, white and pale green parts, thinly sliced, for serving

Put the potatoes in a large pot and add enough cold salted water to cover. Bring to a boil over high heat. Reduce the heat to medium-low, cover, and simmer until the potatoes are tender when pierced with the tip of a sharp knife, 20—25 minutes. Drain and rinse under cold running water. Let stand until cool enough to handle. Slice the potatoes into rounds about ½ inch (12 mm) thick. (The potatoes can be prepared up to 1 day ahead, covered, and refrigerated.)

Preheat the oven to 200°F (95°C). In a large frying pan, preferably cast iron, heat ¼ cup (2 fl oz/60 ml) of the butter over medium-high heat. Add half of the potatoes and cook, stirring occasionally, until golden brown, about 12 minutes. Transfer to a rimmed baking sheet and keep warm in the oven while frying the remaining potatoes in the remaining butter. Combine the two batches in the frying pan. Sprinkle with the paprika, season with salt and pepper, and stir to combine.

Preheat the broiler. Have ready another rimmed baking sheet. Divide the potatoes evenly among 6 heatproof bowls or serving dishes. Top each with about ⅓ cup (3 fl oz/80 ml) of the green chile sauce, then ¼ cup (1 oz/30 g) of the cheese. Arrange the bowls on the baking sheet and broil until the cheese is melted and bubbling, about 1 minute. Top each serving with a dollop of sour cream and a scattering of green onions. Serve at once.

Change it up For a complete meal (not that this isn't substantial on its own), top each serving with some cooked Mexican chorizo sausage or a fried egg.

For many of us, it is unthinkable to eat baked ham without a huge scoop of creamy, cheesy scalloped potatoes alongside. Most old family recipes call for Cheddar cheese and milk, thickened with a sprinkling of flour, but this updated version takes it to a new level, with rich cream, nutty Gruyère, and meltingly tender leeks.

RICH SCALLOPED POTATOES

Makes 8 servings

Unsalted butter, 2 tablespoons, plus more for the baking dish

Leeks, 3 cups (12 oz/ 375 g) chopped, white and pale green parts

Kosher salt, 2 teaspoons

Freshly ground pepper, ½ teaspoon

Baking potatoes, 3¾ pounds (1.85 kg)

Gruyère cheese, 2 cups (8 oz/250 g) shredded

Heavy cream, 3 cups (24 fl oz/750 ml)

Preheat the oven to 350°F (180°C). Generously butter a 9-by-13-inch (23-by-33-cm) baking dish.

In a large frying pan, melt the butter over medium heat. Add the leeks and cook, stirring occasionally, until tender, about 7 minutes. Remove from the heat.

Mix together the salt and pepper. Peel the potatoes and thinly slice into rounds.

Spread one-third of the potatoes in an even layer in the prepared baking dish and season with about one-fourth of the salt mixture. Top with one-third of the Gruyère and half of the leeks and season with about one-third of the remaining salt mixture.

Top with half of the remaining potato slices, half of the remaining Gruyère, and the rest of the leeks, seasoning with half of the remaining salt mixture as you go. Finish with the remaining potatoes and Gruyère and season with the remaining salt mixture.

In a small saucepan, heat the cream over medium-high heat until it is simmering. Pour the hot cream evenly over the potatoes. Cover tightly with aluminum foil and place the baking dish on a rimmed baking sheet.

Bake for 1 hour. Remove the foil and continue baking until the potatoes are tender, coated with a creamy sauce, and golden brown on top, about 30 minutes longer. Let stand for about 5 minutes, then serve hot.

Change it up For the classic all-American version of scalloped potatoes, omit the leeks and substitute sharp white Cheddar cheese for the Gruyère and whole milk for the cream. As you add the potatoes, sprinkle each layer with 1 tablespoon all-purpose flour, for a total of 3 tablespoons.

This updated take of an American classic, made with fresh ingredients, is guaranteed to trump the canned-ingredient version in flavor and nutrition. Here, tender-crisp green beans are coated in a fresh mushroom-cream sauce, and topped with crunchy shallots.

THE ALL-NEW GREEN BEAN CASSEROLE

Makes 6-8 servings

Unsalted butter, 2 tablespoons, plus more for the baking dish

Green beans, 1¼ pounds (625 g)

Kosher salt and freshly ground pepper

Button mushrooms, 10 ounces (315 g), sliced

Shallots, 3 large, plus 3 tablespoons minced

All-purpose flour, ⅓ cup (2 oz/60 g) plus 3 tablespoons

Half-and-half, 1 cup (8 fl oz/250 ml)

Chicken stock (page 212) or broth, 1 cup (8 fl oz/250 ml)

Soy sauce, preferably mushroom soy sauce, 1 teaspoon

Canola oil for deep-frying

Preheat the oven to 350°F (180°C). Lightly butter a deep 2½-quart (2½-l) baking dish. Trim the green beans and halve crosswise. Bring a saucepan of salted water to a boil over high heat. Add the green beans and cook until tender-crisp, about 4 minutes. Drain and rinse under cold running water. Pat dry with paper towels and set aside.

In a saucepan, melt the butter over medium heat. Add the mushrooms and cook, stirring, until they give off their juices and are browned, 6—7 minutes. Stir in the 3 tablespoons minced shallots and cook until softened, 2—3 minutes. Sprinkle with the 3 tablespoons flour and stir well. Slowly stir in the half-and-half, stock, and soy sauce and then bring to a boil, stirring often. Reduce the heat to low and simmer, stirring, until thickened, 4—5 minutes. Stir in the green beans, season with salt and pepper, and transfer the mixture to the prepared baking dish. (The casserole can be prepared to this point up to 1 day ahead, covered, and refrigerated.) Bake until the liquid is bubbling, about 20 minutes (30 minutes if it has been refrigerated).

While the casserole is baking, pour oil to a depth of 2 inches (5 cm) into a heavy saucepan and heat over high heat to 350°F (180°C) on a deep-frying thermometer. Line a baking sheet with paper towels and place near the stove. Cut the remaining 3 shallots crosswise into slices ⅛ inch (3 mm) thick and separate into rings. Place the remaining ⅓ cup (2 oz/60 g) flour in a small bowl. Toss the shallot rings in the flour to coat evenly, shaking off the excess. In batches to avoid crowding, add the shallots to the hot oil and deep-fry until golden brown, about 30 seconds. Transfer to the paper towels to drain. Remove the casserole from the oven, scatter the fried shallots on top, and serve.

Lighten it up Substitute 1 head broccoli (about 1½ pounds/750 g) cut into florets, for the green beans. If you don't feel like frying the shallots, sprinkle ½ cup (2 oz/60 g) toasted sliced almonds over the casserole before serving.

At their best, baked beans, which have been at the center of the American table since colonial times, are both sweet and salty and have a tender bite—all of which add up to comfort food that never goes out of fashion. For the most traditional taste, look for Grade B maple syrup from Vermont.

MAPLE BAKED BEANS

Makes 8 servings

Great Northern or cannellini beans, 1 pound (about 2¼ cups/15¾ oz/500 g)

Kosher salt, 2 teaspoons

Canola oil, 1 tablespoon

Yellow onion, 1 large, chopped

Pure maple syrup, 1 cup (12 fl oz/345 g)

Dark brown sugar, ⅓ cup (2½ oz/75 g) firmly packed

Dry mustard, 1 teaspoon

Salt pork, ¾ pound (375 g)

Rinse the beans and pick them over, discarding any misshapen beans or stones. In a large bowl, combine the beans with water to cover by 1 inch (2.5 cm), and let stand at cool room temperature for at least 4 hours or up to 12 hours. (If the weather is warm, refrigerate the beans while soaking.)

Drain the beans, transfer to a large saucepan, and add water to cover. Cover and bring to a boil over high heat. Set the lid askew, reduce the heat to medium-low, and simmer until the beans are barely tender, 30—40 minutes. Stir in the salt during the last 10 minutes of cooking.

Meanwhile, in a large frying pan, heat the oil over medium heat. Add the onion and cook, stirring occasionally, until softened, about 5 minutes. Reduce the heat to low and cook, stirring occasionally, until the onion is very tender and turns a deep golden brown, about 25 minutes. Remove from the heat.

When the beans are ready, drain them in a colander, reserving the cooking liquid. Transfer the beans to a bowl. Add the cooked onion, maple syrup, brown sugar, and mustard and stir to combine.

Preheat the oven to 325°F (165°C). Trim off and discard the rind from the salt pork, then thinly slice. Line the bottom of a deep 2½- to 3-quart (2½- to 3-l) baking dish or Dutch oven with one-third of the salt pork. Add half of the beans, then half of the remaining salt pork. Top with the remaining beans and salt pork. Add enough of the reserved cooking liquid to barely cover the beans. Cover and bake for 2 hours. Uncover and continue baking until the cooking liquid has thickened to a glossy syrup, about 1½ hours more. Remove from the oven and let stand for 5 minutes. Serve hot.

Change it up   If you can't find salt pork, use thick bacon slices, preferably applewood smoked. Or, bury a smoked ham hock or smoked turkey wing in the beans before you put them in the oven.

This mac and cheese is miles away from its neon-boxed cousin that you may have had as a kid. Once you have enjoyed a plate of this from-scratch version, bubbling hot from the oven, with its flavorful cheeses and buttery crown of crisp bread crumbs, you will be hard-pressed to return to its store-bought kin.

CREAMY MAC & CHEESE

Makes 6 servings

Unsalted butter, 7 tablespoons (3½ oz/ 105 g), plus more for the baking dish

Garlic, 1 clove, minced

Coarse fresh bread crumbs, 1½ cups (3 oz/90 g)

Kosher salt and freshly ground pepper

Elbow macaroni, 1 pound (500 g)

All-purpose flour, ¼ cup (1½ oz/45 g)

Whole milk, 3 cups (24 fl oz/750 ml), warmed

Sharp Cheddar cheese, 2 cups (8 oz/250 g) shredded

Fontina cheese, 2 cups (8 oz/250 g) shredded

Dry mustard, ½ teaspoon

In a large frying pan, melt 3 tablespoons of the butter over medium-low heat. Add the garlic and cook, stirring frequently, until tender but not browned, about 3 minutes. Add the bread crumbs and stir until coated with butter. Set aside.

Preheat the oven to 350°F (180°C). Butter a shallow 3-quart (3-l) baking dish.

Bring a large pot of lightly salted water to a boil over high heat. Add the macaroni and stir occasionally until the water returns to a boil. Cook according to the package directions until not quite al dente. (The macaroni will cook again in the oven, so do not overcook it now.) Drain well and set aside.

Add the remaining 4 tablespoons (2 oz/60 g) butter to the pot used for the pasta and melt over medium heat. Whisk in the flour. Reduce the heat to medium-low and let bubble for 1 minute without browning. Gradually whisk in the milk, raise the heat to medium, and bring to a boil, whisking frequently. Remove from the heat and stir in the cheeses along with the mustard. Season with salt and pepper. Stir in the pasta. Spread in the prepared baking dish and sprinkle evenly with the buttered crumbs.

Bake until the crumbs are browned and the sauce is bubbling, about 20 minutes. Let cool for 5 minutes, then serve hot.

Change it up Any tubular pasta will do: try penne, ziti, or mostaccioli. To give your mac and cheese a little personality, add chopped crisp bacon, cubes of smoked ham or cooked chicken, cooked peas, chopped blanched broccoli, sautéed wild mushrooms, or crumbled blue cheese.

Perhaps the reigning king of all comfort food side dishes, fluffy mounds of mashed potatoes are delicious served with stews, roasts, and more. Insure they hold up their reputation by paying special attention to the details: using the right potatoes, warming the milk so the potatoes don't cool, and adding lots of sweet butter.

BUTTERY MASHED POTATOES

Makes 6 servings

Baking potatoes,
3 pounds (1.5 kg)

Kosher salt and freshly ground white pepper

Unsalted butter,
½ cup (4 oz/125 g), at room temperature plus more for serving

Whole milk, about ½ cup (4 fl oz/125 ml), warmed

Fresh chives,
3 tablespoons minced

Peel the potatoes and cut into chunks. In a large saucepan, combine the potatoes with salted water to cover, cover the pan, and bring to a boil over high heat.

Uncover, reduce the heat to medium-low, and simmer until the potatoes are tender when pierced with a knife, about 20 minutes. Drain well. Return the potatoes to the pan and stir over medium-low heat for 2 minutes to evaporate the excess moisture.

Press the warm potatoes through a ricer into a large bowl. Cut the butter into slices and scatter over the potatoes. Whisk in the butter and enough of the milk to give the potatoes the texture you like. (Or, if you don't have a ricer, beat the potatoes in the pot with a handheld mixer on high speed. Add the butter and continue beating on high speed, adding milk as needed to create the desired texture. Be careful not to overbeat the potatoes.)

Mix in the chives and season to taste with salt and pepper. Transfer to a warmed serving bowl and serve at once with additional butter, if desired.

Change it up
Give the mashed potatoes a boost of flavor with roasted garlic. Slice a head of garlic in half crosswise, drizzle the halves with olive oil, wrap them in aluminum foil, and place in a small, shallow pan. Bake in a preheated 400°F (200°C) oven until the cloves are soft, about 35 minutes. Squeeze the cloves from their papery sheaths into the potatoes when you add the milk and whisk to combine.

These soufflés are from the big family of warm, comforting cheese dishes. They are made with rich, tangy fresh goat cheese—be sure to use a rindless one—and rise beautifully in the oven, with the center forming a little "top hat." Serve alongside roast lamb for a feast, or pair with a green salad for a simple but special meal.

CHEESE SOUFFLÉS

Makes 6 servings

Unsalted butter,
2 tablespoons
plus 1 teaspoon, plus
more for the ramekins

Parmesan cheese,
3 tablespoons freshly
grated

Garlic, 1 clove, minced

All-purpose flour,
3 tablespoons

Whole milk, 1 cup
(8 fl oz/250 ml), warmed

Fresh goat cheese,
6 ounces (185 g)

Fresh thyme,
½ teaspoon minced

Fine sea salt,
⅛ teaspoon

Freshly ground pepper,
¼ teaspoon

Large eggs, 4, separated,
plus 1 egg white

Preheat the oven to 375°F (190°C). Lightly butter six ¾-cup (6-fl oz/180-ml) ramekins, then sprinkle with the Parmesan, tilt to coat the sides evenly with cheese, and tap out the excess.

In a saucepan, melt the 2 tablespoons butter over medium heat. Add the garlic and cook, stirring frequently, until fragrant but not browned, about 1 minute. Whisk in the flour. Reduce the heat to medium-low and let bubble for 1 minute without browning. Gradually whisk in the milk, raise the heat to medium, and bring to a boil, whisking frequently. Reduce the heat to medium-low and cook, whisking frequently, until very thick, about 3 minutes. Remove from the heat, crumble in the goat cheese, and whisk until it melts. Whisk in the thyme, salt, and pepper. Cut the 1 teaspoon butter into small pieces and dot the top of the cheese mixture. (The cheese mixture can be prepared up to 1 hour ahead and covered tightly. Reheat over low heat, whisking often, before proceeding.)

In a large bowl, whisk the egg yolks until blended. Gradually whisk the warm cheese mixture into the yolks. In another bowl, using a handheld mixer on high speed, beat the 5 egg whites until soft peaks form. Stir about one-fourth of the beaten egg whites into the yolk mixture to lighten it, then gently fold in the remaining whites just until combined. Divide the mixture evenly among the prepared ramekins, filling each one about three-fourths full. One at a time, insert a butter knife into each soufflé mixture and trace a circle about 1 inch (2.5 cm) deep and ¼ inch (6 mm) from the sides of the ramekin. (This creates the "top hat.")

Place the ramekins on a baking sheet and bake until the tops are puffed and golden brown and the soufflés quiver gently when jostled (the insides will be lightly set, and maybe a bit soft), about 20 minutes. Serve at once.

Change it up   Have fun experimenting with different types of cheeses and herbs. For example, substitute 1 cup (4 oz/125 g) shredded sharp Cheddar or Gruyère cheese for the goat cheese. Rosemary is a good substitute for the thyme.

California is artichoke country, and many locals boil them up and eat them with plenty of melted butter or mayonnaise for dipping. This Italian-American version of stuffed artichokes, with a garlicky filling of bread crumbs and pine nuts, showcases the best way to eat these unique vegetables, without drowning them in fats.

STUFFED ARTICHOKES

Makes 4 servings

Lemon, 1, halved crosswise

Artichokes, 4 (about 9 ounces/280 g each), with stems attached

Olive oil, 6 tablespoons (3 fl oz/90 ml)

Coarse fresh bread crumbs, 2 cups (4 oz/120 g)

Pine nuts, ⅓ cup (¼ oz/50 g), toasted

Fresh flat-leaf parsley, 2 tablespoons minced

Garlic, 3 cloves, minced

Dried oregano, ½ teaspoon

Kosher salt and freshly ground pepper

Mayonnaise (page 216 or purchased) for serving

Squeeze the juice from 1 lemon half into a bowl, add 6 cups (48 fl oz/1.5 l) cold water, and then add the squeezed lemon half. Cut off the stem from each artichoke at the base. Rub the cut areas with the remaining lemon half. Using a paring knife, trim away the thick skin from each stem. Rub the peeled stems with the lemon half, then dice.

Add 1 tablespoon of the olive oil to a frying pan and heat over medium heat. Add the diced stems and ¼ cup (2 fl oz/60 ml) water, reduce the heat to medium-low, cover, and cook until the stems are tender and the water has evaporated, 8–10 minutes. Let cool slightly.

Meanwhile, cut 1 inch (2.5 cm) off the top of each artichoke. Using kitchen scissors, snip off any thorny tips that remain on the leaves. Rub the cut areas with the lemon half. One at a time, place the artichokes upside down on a work surface. Press hard on the artichoke bottom with the heel of your hand to loosen the leaves and force them far enough apart to hold the stuffing.

In a bowl, combine the bread crumbs, cooked stems, pine nuts, parsley, garlic, and oregano. Stir in 2 tablespoons of the olive oil. Season with salt and pepper. Using one-fourth of the bread crumb mixture for each artichoke, stuff the mixture between the outer few layers of thick leaves. Leave the thin inner leaves intact.

Pour 1 tablespoon of the olive oil into a saucepan just large enough to hold the artichokes upright in a single layer, and tilt to coat the pan bottom. Arrange the stuffed artichokes, bases down, in the saucepan and drizzle with the remaining 2 tablespoons olive oil. Add water to come ½ inch (12 mm) up the sides of the artichokes without immersing the stuffing. Bring to a boil over high heat. Reduce the heat to medium-low, cover, and simmer, adding more boiling water to the pan as needed to maintain the level, until a leaf can be easily pulled from an artichoke, about 1 hour.

Meanwhile, preheat the oven to 400°F (200°C). Lightly oil a rimmed baking sheet. When the artichokes are ready, using tongs, carefully transfer the artichokes, bases down, to the baking sheet. Bake until the stuffing is lightly browned, about 15 minutes. Transfer each artichoke to an individual bowl and serve with the mayonnaise.

For many of us, creamed spinach recalls special-occasion dinners at white-tablecloth steakhouses. We somehow forget to make this dish at home, but with shallots, garlic, and Parmesan cheese, this recipe will hold its own next to grilled steaks and roasts, possibly even more so than your favorite restaurant version.

CREAMED SPINACH

Makes 6 servings

Spinach, 3½ pounds (1.75 kg)

Heavy cream, 1 cup (8 fl oz/250 ml)

Whole milk, 1 cup (8 fl oz/250 ml)

Unsalted butter, 3 tablespoons

Shallots, ¼ cup (1½ oz/45 g) minced

Garlic, 1 clove, minced

All-purpose flour, 3 tablespoons

Parmesan cheese, ½ cup (2 oz/60 g) freshly grated

Kosher salt and freshly ground pepper

Freshly grated nutmeg

Remove the stems from the spinach leaves and chop the leaves coarsely. Fill the sink or a large bowl with cold water. Add the spinach and swirl it in the water to loosen any grit. Transfer the spinach, with any water clinging to it, to a large bowl.

In a large saucepan, bring ½ cup (4 fl oz/125 ml) water to a boil over high heat. In batches, add the spinach to the pan and cover, letting each batch wilt before adding the next one. Cook until the spinach is tender, about 5 minutes. Drain the spinach in a large coarse-mesh sieve, then rinse briefly under cold running water. Let cool until easy to handle. A handful at a time, squeeze the spinach to remove any excess water and place in a bowl. Set aside.

In a small saucepan, bring the cream and milk to a simmer over medium heat. Remove from the heat. In the large saucepan you used for the spinach, melt the butter over medium heat. Add the shallots and garlic and cook, stirring frequently, until the shallots soften, about 2 minutes. Whisk in the flour. Reduce the heat to medium-low and let bubble for 1 minute. Gradually whisk in the hot cream mixture, raise the heat to medium, and bring to a boil, whisking frequently. Reduce the heat to medium-low and simmer until lightly thickened, about 5 minutes. Stir in the spinach and cook until heated through, about 5 minutes more.

Whisk in the Parmesan, and season with salt, pepper, and a pinch of the nutmeg. Transfer to a warmed serving dish and serve at once.

Change it up Just before serving, top the creamed spinach with a generous sprinkling of crisp-cooked chopped bacon or pancetta. You can make it even more hearty by adding mushrooms, such as button, cremini, or shiitake. Sauté 1 cup (3 oz/90 g) sliced mushrooms in 1 tablespoon unsalted butter until lightly browned, about 5 minutes. Add to the sauce along with the spinach.

Collard greens are quite bitter, but southern cooks know how to tame them. They lose their edge when simmered with smoky bacon and pungent garlic, and are perked up by a splash of vinegar and a shake of red pepper. The best part of a pot of greens is sopping up the cooking liquid with a thick wedge of Cornbread (page 172).

COLLARD GREENS WITH BACON

Makes 6-8 servings

Collard greens, 4 pounds (2 kg)

Applewood-smoked bacon, 6 thick slices, coarsely chopped

Canola oil, 1 tablespoon

Garlic, 4 cloves, minced

Red pepper flakes, ¼ teaspoon

Cider vinegar, 2 tablespoons, plus more for serving

Kosher salt

Trim off and discard the thick stems from the collard greens. In batches, stack the leaves and cut crosswise into strips about ½ inch (12 mm) wide. Fill the sink or a large bowl with cold water. Add the greens and swirl them to loosen any grit. Transfer the collard greens, with any water clinging to them, to a large bowl.

In a large pot or a large, deep sauté pan, fry the bacon in the oil over medium heat until browned and crisp, about 8 minutes. Using a slotted spoon, transfer the bacon to paper towels to drain. Remove the pot from the heat, with the bacon fat still in it, and let cool slightly.

Return the pot to medium-low heat. Add the garlic and cook, stirring frequently, until softened, about 1 minute. Increase the heat to medium-high. Add a handful of the collard greens to the pot, cover, and cook until they wilt. Continue adding the greens, a handful at a time and allowing them to wilt before adding the next batch, until all of the greens are in the pot. Add the red pepper flakes, cover, reduce the heat to medium-low, and simmer, stirring occasionally, for about 15 minutes if you like the greens tender but still fresh, or up to 45 minutes if you like them well done.

Stir in the reserved bacon and the 2 tablespoons vinegar. Season with salt, then taste and adjust with red pepper flakes. Transfer the greens and their cooking liquid to a warmed serving bowl. Serve hot, passing vinegar on the side.

Lighten it up Other greens, such as dandelion, mustard, and kale, can be cooked in the same way, or you can use a combination of greens. Instead of using bacon, sauté the garlic in 2 tablespoons olive oil, bury a smoked ham hock or a smoked turkey wing in the greens, and cook for about 1½ hours to allow the meat to infuse the greens with smoky flavor. Don't worry: they can take the extended heat.

Naturally sweet roasted root vegetables are a delicious counterpoint to the smoky and salty flavors of crisp bacon or sliced ham. With the exception of beets, which will stain other ingredients, use any combination of cubed vegetables you like, from crispy-edged potatoes to sweet carrots and parsnips to earthy celery root.

ROASTED ROOT VEGETABLES WITH FRESH THYME

Makes 6-8 servings

Olive oil, 3 tablespoons plus more for the pan

Yukon gold potatoes, 4 (about 1½ lb/750 g total weight), peeled and cut into cubes

Parsnips, 2 (about ½ lb/250 g total weight), peeled and cut into cubes

Carrots, 2 large, peeled and cut into cubes, tops reserved for serving (optional)

Celery Root, 1, peeled and cut into cubes

Yellow onions, 2, cut lengthwise into quarters

Fennel, 2, cut lengthwise into quarters

Fresh thyme, 1½ teaspoons minced

Kosher salt and freshly ground pepper

Preheat the oven to 425°F (220°C). Lightly oil a large roasting pan. In a large bowl, toss the potatoes, parsnips, carrots, and celery root with 2 tablespoons of the oil to coat. Spread in the prepared pan. Bake until the vegetables begin to soften, about 25 minutes.

Toss the onion wedges with the remaining 1 tablespoon oil, trying to keep the wedges intact. Remove the roasting pan from the oven and turn the vegetables over with a metal spatula. Nestle the onion wedges and fennel among the vegetables in the pan. Continue roasting until the vegetables are very tender and their edges are tinged dark brown, about 25 minutes more.

Sprinkle the roasted vegetables with the thyme, season with salt and pepper, and toss gently. Sprinkle the carrot tops over the top, if using. Serve at once.

Change it up To glaze the root vegetables, drizzle them with 3 tablespoons pure maple syrup during the last 5 minutes of roasting, and turn to coat. You can also cut the vegetables into matchsticks or thick wedges.

Nowadays, potato salad often seems to arrive with all sorts of "new" ingredients, which might be tasty, but just don't evoke the simple dish you remember. For those of you who think old ways are often the best ways, here is a recipe that makes nearly everyone reminiscent about family picnics and grandmother's potato salad.

OLD-FASHIONED POTATO SALAD

Makes 8 servings

Red-skinned potatoes, 3 pounds (1.5 kg)

Kosher salt and freshly ground pepper

White wine vinegar, 3 tablespoons

Mayonnaise (page 216 or purchased), 1 cup (8 fl oz/250 ml)

Whole-grain mustard, 2 tablespoons

Celery, 4 stalks, finely diced

Green onions, 4, white and green parts, chopped

Fresh flat-leaf parsley, 2 tablespoons minced

Place the unpeeled potatoes in a large saucepan, add salted water to cover by 1 inch (2.5 cm), cover, and bring to a boil over high heat. Set the lid askew, reduce the heat to medium-low, and cook at a brisk simmer until the potatoes are tender, about 25 minutes. Drain, then rinse the potatoes under cold running water until they are cool enough to handle.

Cut the potatoes into chunks about ½ inch (12 mm) thick and place in a large bowl. Sprinkle with the vinegar. Let cool completely.

In a small bowl, mix together the mayonnaise and mustard. Add to the potatoes along with the celery, green onions, and parsley and mix gently. Season with salt and pepper. Cover and refrigerate until chilled, at least 2 hours. Serve chilled.

Change it up If you like hard-boiled eggs in your potato salad, by all means, add them. The same goes for chopped dill pickles or bread-and-butter pickles—you can even use pickle juice in place of the vinegar. You can also cook baking potatoes instead of red-skinned ones. They fall apart more easily, but some folks like that.

Many barbecue aficionados argue that a barbecue isn't a barbecue without a big bowl of cool, crisp coleslaw on the table. Indeed, nothing tastes better alongside a batch of spicy barbecued ribs. If you turn up your nose at too-sweet slaws, this one is for you. It gets its subtle sweetness from an unexpected source—grated apple.

CREAMY COLESLAW

Makes 6-8 servings

Green cabbage, 1 head (about 2 pounds/1 kg)

Celery, 2 stalks

Granny Smith apple, 1

Yellow or red onion, 1 small

Carrots, 2 small, peeled

Cider vinegar, 2 tablespoons

Fresh flat-leaf parsley, 2 tablespoons minced

Mayonnaise (page 216 or purchased), 1¼ cups (10 fl oz/300 ml)

Kosher salt and freshly ground pepper

Cut the cabbage into wedges through the stem end, and cut out the core. Using a food processor or a stand mixer fitted with the thin slicing attachment, slice the cabbage into thin slivers. Transfer to a large bowl. Slice the celery with the slicing disk, and add it to the cabbage.

Replace the slicing attachment with the shredding attachment. Halve and core the apple but do not peel. Cut the apple and the onion into wedges. Shred the apple, onion, and carrots, and add to the cabbage and celery.

Sprinkle the vegetables with the vinegar and toss to coat evenly. Add the parsley and mayonnaise and mix well. Season with salt and pepper. Cover and refrigerate until chilled, at least 2 hours. Taste and adjust the seasoning with more vinegar, salt, and pepper before serving. Serve cold.

Change it up If you don't have a food processor, you can ready the vegetables by hand with a chef's knife and box shredder-grater. And if you prefer a sweeter coleslaw, stir in a bit of sugar until the flavor suits you. Thinly sliced red bell pepper and cucumber are also nice additions.

Biting into hot corn on the cob slathered with butter is one of summer's great eating pleasures. Here, that classic is given a fresh, Latin accent with the addition of lime and cilantro to the butter and a sprinkle of ground chile at the table. Be careful not to overcook the corn, it tastes best when the kernels still carry some snap.

MEXICAN-STYLE CORN ON THE COB

Makes 6 servings

Cilantro-Lime Butter

Unsalted butter, ½ cup (4 oz/125 g), at room temperature

Fresh cilantro, 2 tablespoons minced

Finely grated lime zest, from 1 lime

Fresh lime juice, 1 tablespoon

Fresh corn, 6 ears

Pure ancho chile powder or other chile powder for serving

Kosher salt

To make the cilantro-lime butter, using a rubber spatula, in a small bowl, mash together the butter, cilantro, and lime zest and juice. Cover and let stand while you prepare the corn. (The butter can be prepared, covered, and refrigerated for up to 2 days. Bring to room temperature before serving.)

Remove the husks and silk from the ears of corn. Bring a large pot of water to a boil over high heat. Add the corn and cook until the kernels are tender-crisp, about 5 minutes. Drain well and transfer to a serving platter. Serve the corn piping hot, with the cilantro-lime butter, chile powder, and salt on the side for diners to add as they like.

Change it up In Mexico, corn on the cob is often spread with crema (similar to sour cream) or mayonnaise, sprinkled with shredded cotija cheese, and seasoned with pure ground chile and a squeeze of lime juice.

The scent of freshly baked rolls wafting from the oven is only matched by their old-fashioned flavor. Enriched with egg, milk, and butter, these are so light that they will threaten to float off your plate. A roll is just as good plain, with just a pat of butter, or used to sop up gravy from a roast off the plate.

TENDER DINNER ROLLS

Makes 9 rolls

Active dry yeast, 2¼ teaspoons

Warm water (105° to 115°F/40°C to 46°C), ¼ cup (2 fl oz/60 ml)

Cold water, ½ cup (5 fl oz/160 ml)

Whole milk, ¼ cup (2 fl oz/60 ml), heated to steaming

Unsalted butter, 2 tablespoons, melted and cooled

Sugar, 1 tablespoon

Large egg yolk, 1

Kosher salt, 1½ teaspoons

Unbleached all-purpose flour, 3 cups (15 oz/470 g)

Softened butter, for the bowl and baking pan

Whole milk, 1 tablespoon, for brushing

Sesame sesame seeds or poppy seeds, 1 teaspoon, for garnish

In a small bowl, sprinkle the yeast over the warm water. Let it stand for 5 minutes, then stir to dissolve the yeast. Mix the cold water and hot milk together in the bowl of a heavy stand mixer (or a large bowl) to cool the milk to tepid. Add the dissolved yeast, melted butter, sugar, egg yolk, and salt. On low speed, with the paddle attachment, mix in enough of the flour to make a soft dough that cleans the sides of the bowl. (Or, using a wooden spoon, stir in enough flour to make a dough that cannot be stirred.) Change to the dough hook and mix on medium-low speed, adding more flour as needed, until the dough is smooth, elastic, and tacky, about 6 minutes. (Or turn out the dough onto a lightly floured work surface and knead by hand, adding more flour as needed, about 8 minutes.) The dough should be soft, so do not add too much flour.)

Lightly butter a medium bowl. Shape the dough into a ball. Put the dough in the bowl, turn the ball to coat it, and leave smooth side up. Cover the bowl with plastic wrap. Let stand in a warm place until it is doubled in volume, about 1 hour. (This dough rises more quickly than ones with less sugar.)

Lightly butter an 11½-by-8-inch (29-by-20-cm) baking dish. Turn the dough out onto an unfloured work surface and knead briefly. Divide the dough into 12 equal pieces. Shape each into a taut ball. Place the balls, smooth sides up, equally spaced, in the baking dish. Cover loosely the dish with plastic wrap and let stand in a warm place until almost doubled in volume, about 30 minutes.

Position a rack in the center of the oven and preheat the oven to 350°F (180°C). Lightly brush the tops of the balls with some of the milk and sprinkle with the seeds. Bake until the rolls are fully risen and golden brown, 25 to 30 minutes. Remove from the oven and let cool in the pan for 10 minutes. Serve warm or cooled to room temperature.

Crisp on the outside and tender on the inside, these flaky biscuits are so easy to prepare that you'll be tempted to whip up a batch to serve with every meal, be it a hearty breakfast of fried eggs and Creamy Grits (page 213), a hot soup lunch, or at supper alongside sliced baked ham.

BUTTERMILK BISCUITS

Makes 6-8 biscuits

All-purpose flour, 1 cup (5 oz/155 g)

Cake flour, 1 cup (4 oz/125 g)

Baking powder, 2 teaspoons

Baking soda, ½ teaspoon

Kosher salt, ½ teaspoon

Unsalted butter, 6 tablespoons (3 oz/90 g), chilled

Buttermilk, ¾ cup (6 fl oz/180 ml)

Butter and honey for serving (optional)

Preheat the oven to 400°F (200°C). Have ready an ungreased rimmed baking sheet.

In a bowl, sift together the flours, baking powder, baking soda, and salt. Cut the butter into tablespoons and scatter over the flour mixture. Using a pastry blender or 2 knives, cut the butter into the flour mixture just until the mixture forms coarse crumbs the size of peas. Add the buttermilk and stir just until the dough comes together. Knead the dough a few times in the bowl.

Turn out the dough onto a lightly floured work surface. Using a light touch, pat out the dough into a round ¾ inch (2 cm) thick. Using a 2½-inch (6-cm) round biscuit cutter or cookie cutter, cut out as many rounds as possible. Place them 1 inch (2.5 cm) apart on the baking sheet. Gather up the dough scraps, pat them out again, cut out more dough rounds, and add them to the baking sheet. Bake the biscuits until they have risen and are golden brown, 18–20 minutes. Serve hot with butter and honey, if desired.

Change it up For savory biscuits, stir ½ cup (2 oz/60 g) shredded sharp Cheddar cheese, 1½ tablespoons minced fresh chives, and ¼ teaspoon freshly ground pepper into the flour and butter mixture before adding the buttermilk. You may need to use a little more buttermilk. The biscuits won't rise as high, but they will still be delicious.

This not-too-sweet cornbread has earned a place at my breakfast table as the ultimate partner to eggs and spicy sausage. Lightly sweetened with maple syrup and flecked with corn kernels, chunks of mild poblano chiles, and bits of sharp Cheddar cheese, then baked in a cast-iron skillet, it isn't your everyday cornbread.

CHEESE & CHILE SKILLET CORNBREAD

Makes 8 servings

Poblano chile, 2

All-purpose flour, 1 cup
(5 oz/155 g)

**Yellow cornmeal,
preferably stone-ground,**
1 cup (7 oz/220 g)

Baking powder,
2 teaspoons

Fine sea salt, ½ teaspoon

Unsalted butter, ¼ cup
(2 oz/60 g)

Whole milk, ¾ cup
(6 fl oz/180 ml)

Pure maple syrup, ¼ cup
(3 oz/90 g)

Egg, 1 large, beaten

Sharp Cheddar cheese,
1 cup (4 oz/125 g)
shredded

**Fresh or thawed frozen
corn kernels,** 1 cup
(6 oz/185 g)

Preheat the broiler. Place the chiles on a baking sheet and broil, turning occasionally, until the skins are blackened on all sides, about 12 minutes. Transfer to a cutting board and let cool until easy to handle. Peel off the blackened skin. Discard the stem, seeds, and ribs, and chop the chiles.

Preheat the oven to 400°F (200°C). In a bowl, sift together the flour, cornmeal, baking powder, and salt. Make a well in the center of the flour mixture.

Place the butter in a 10-inch (25-cm) heatproof frying pan, preferably cast iron. Place in the oven until the butter is melted, about 3 minutes. Remove the pan from the oven and pour 2 tablespoons of the melted butter into a large bowl, leaving the remaining butter in the pan and tilting the pan to coat. Add the milk, maple syrup, and egg to the butter in the bowl and stir to combine. Pour the milk mixture into the well in the flour mixture and stir just until combined. Fold in the chopped chile, cheese, and corn. Spread the batter in the hot pan.

Bake until the cornbread is golden brown and a toothpick inserted into the center comes out clean, about 30 minutes. Transfer to a wire rack and let cool in the pan for 5 minutes. Cut into wedges and serve hot or warm.

Once you have tasted this dish of sweet, milky corn, made from fresh kernels, you will never reach for its canned namesake again. Use only farm-fresh ears of corn here, and use them soon after you bring them home, before their natural sugars have the time to turn to starch.

CREAMED CORN

Makes 4 servings

Fresh corn, 6 ears

Unsalted butter, 2 tablespoons

Yellow onion, 1 small, finely chopped

Sugar, ½ teaspoon

Kosher salt and freshly ground pepper

Heavy cream, ¾ cup (6 fl oz/180 ml)

Fresh chives, 2 tablespoons minced

Remove the husks and silk from the ears of corn. Using a chef's knife, cut each ear in half crosswise. One at a time, stand the halves cut side down on a cutting board and slice the kernels from the cobs. Transfer the kernels to a bowl. Using the dull edge of the knife blade, scrape the milk and pulp from the corn cobs into the bowl.

In a large frying pan, melt the butter over medium heat. Add the onion and cook, stirring occasionally, until translucent, 5–6 minutes. Add the corn kernels with the pulp, the sugar, and ½ cup (4 fl oz/125 ml) water, and season with salt and pepper. Bring to a boil, reduce the heat to low, cover, and cook, stirring occasionally, until the corn is tender but still has a bit of crunch, 8–10 minutes. Uncover and cook until the water evaporates, 2–3 minutes.

Add the cream to the pan, raise the heat to medium, and cook until the cream has thickened enough to coat the back of a spoon, about 3 minutes. Stir in the chives.

Transfer to a warmed serving bowl and serve at once.

Change it up Smoky flavor pairs wonderfully with the natural sweetness of corn. In a frying pan, fry 3 slices of bacon, coarsely chopped, over medium heat until crisp, about 7 minutes, then drain on paper towels. Use the bacon fat in place of the butter, and sprinkle the bacon over the corn just before serving. Or, for a version with smoke and spice, add 1 chipotle chile in adobo sauce, seeded and minced, and ½ teaspoon adobo sauce with the cream.

You can steam butternut squash, but the result doesn't hold a candle to thick chunks of squash that are roasted until caramelized and meltingly tender. When cloaked with nutty brown butter and crispy fried sage, it brings up visions of autumn. This scrumptious and healthy squash is excellent alongside pork.

ROASTED BUTTERNUT SQUASH WITH BROWN BUTTER & SAGE

Makes 6-8 servings

Butternut squash, 1 (about 3¼ pounds/ 1.35 kg)

Olive oil, 1 tablespoon

Kosher salt and freshly ground pepper

Unsalted butter, 2 tablespoons

Fresh sage, 24 leaves

Preheat the oven to 425°F (220°C). Using a sturdy vegetable peeler, peel the squash. Using a large, sharp knife, cut the squash crosswise where the bulbous part meets the narrower part, and trim off the blossom and stem ends. Cut the bulbous part in half vertically and scrape out and discard the seeds and fibers. Cut all of the squash into 1-inch (2.5-cm) chunks. Spread the pieces on a rimmed baking sheet. Drizzle with the oil and toss with your hands to coat. Season with salt and pepper.

Roast for 15 minutes. Stir the squash and continue roasting until tender and browned, 10–15 minutes more. Remove from the oven.

In a small frying pan, melt the butter over medium heat until the foam subsides. Add the sage and cook just until the butter turns a light hazelnut brown and the sage is crisp, about 30 seconds. Immediately pour the brown butter and sage over the squash on the baking sheet and toss to coat. Transfer to a warmed serving bowl and serve.

Change it up Root vegetables, such as carrots, potatoes, parsnips, and turnips are also delicious served with brown butter and sage. Cut them all into 1-inch (2.5-cm) chunks. You can roast them together, mixing and matching the vegetables to suit your taste.

DESSERTS

You may have memories of finding small, individually wrapped pies tucked into your school lunch box. And while everyone has his or her favorite pie, surely blueberry is at or near the top of most lists. Be sure to have plenty of napkins ready, as part of the appeal is the delicious fruit juice that runs down your hands.

BLUEBERRY HAND PIES

Makes 6 hand pies

Blueberries, 2 cups (8 oz/250 g)

Sugar, ¼ cup (2 oz/60 g) plus 1 tablespoon

Fresh lemon juice, 1 tablespoon

Cornstarch, 2 teaspoons

Double recipe of Flaky Pastry Dough (page 217)

Flour for dusting

Large egg, 1

In a saucepan, combine 1½ cups (6 oz/200 g) of the blueberries, the ¼ cup (2 oz/60 g) sugar, and lemon juice over medium heat and cook, stirring frequently, until the berries begin to give off their juices. Reduce the heat to medium-low and simmer, stirring occasionally, until all of the berries have burst, about 5 minutes.

Meanwhile, in a small bowl, stir together the cornstarch and 2 tablespoons water. Add the cornstarch mixture to the blueberry mixture and cook until the juices come to a boil and thicken. Remove from the heat and stir in the remaining ½ cup (2 oz/60 g) berries. Place the saucepan in a bowl of ice water and let the mixture cool, stirring frequently.

Preheat the oven to 375°F (190°C). Have ready an ungreased rimmed baking sheet. Place the dough on a lightly floured work surface and divide in half. (If the dough is chilled hard, let it stand at room temperature for a few minutes until it begins to soften before rolling it out.)

One at a time, roll out a dough half into rectangles about 12 by 10 inches (30 by 25 cm) and ⅛ inch (3 mm) thick each. Trim the edges evenly. Using a paring knife, cut each pastry sheet into 3 rectangles measuring 10 by 4 inches (25 by 10 cm). Place about 3 tablespoons of the blueberry filling on one-half of a rectangle, leaving a ½-inch (12-mm) border uncovered. For each pie, with a long side facing you, fold the dough in half vertically so the edges meet, then crimp on all sides with a fork. Transfer to the baking sheet.

In a bowl, beat the egg with 1 teaspoon water to make an egg wash. Lightly brush the pies with the egg wash, cut an X in the top of each pie, and sprinkle with the remaining 1 tablespoon sugar. Bake the pies until golden brown, about 20 minutes. Let the pies cool on the pan on a wire rack, then serve warm or at room temperature.

Change it up To make a simple glaze, sift 1 cup (4 oz/125 g) confectioners' sugar into a bowl and whisk in 1–2 tablespoons water until the mixture has the consistency of heavy cream. Brush the icing over the cooled pies, then let set for a few minutes before serving.

If you love billowy meringue, this is the pie for you. Fragrant Meyer lemons are becoming more widely available, so use them if they are around, although no one will turn down a slice of this pie if you use regular lemons. If pressed for time, store-bought graham cracker crust can be used.

MILE-HIGH LEMON MERINGUE PIE

Makes 8 servings

GRAHAM CRACKER CRUST

Softened butter, for the pie plate

Graham crackers, 1 cup (4 ounces/125 g) crushed

Unsalted butter, 2 tablespoons, melted

Sugar, 2 tablespoons

Large eggs, 8

Sugar, 2 cups (1 lb/500 g) plus 2 tablespoons

Cornstarch, ¼ cup (1 oz/30 g)

Fresh Meyer lemon juice, 1 cup (8 fl oz/250 ml)

Fine sea salt, ¼ teaspoon

Unsalted butter, 4 tablespoons (2 oz/60 g), cut into tablespoons

Finely grated Meyer lemon zest, from 3 lemons

To make the crust, position a rack in the center of the oven and preheat the oven to 350°F (180°C). Lightly butter a 9-inch (23-cm) pie plate.

In a medium bowl, stir the graham crackers, melted butter, and sugar together until moistened. Press firmly and evenly into the pie plate (the flat bottom of a measuring up works well as an aide). Place the pie dish on a rimmed baking sheet. Bake until the crust looks and smells toasty, 10 to 15 minutes. Cool completely.

In a bowl, beat 3 of the eggs until blended. Separate the remaining 5 eggs, adding the yolks to the beaten whole eggs and putting the whites in a separate large bowl.

Cover the whites and set aside at room temperature. Beat the yolks into the beaten eggs. In another bowl, whisk together 1½ cups (12 oz/375 g) of the sugar and the cornstarch, then whisk in the beaten eggs, the lemon juice, and salt. Transfer to a heavy, nonreactive saucepan, place over medium heat, and heat until the mixture comes to a full boil, whisking almost constantly. Reduce the heat to low and let bubble for 30 seconds. Be careful not to undercook or overcook the filling or it will separate as it cools. Remove from the heat and whisk in the butter. Strain through a coarse-mesh sieve into a bowl to remove any bits of cooked egg white. Stir in the lemon zest, then pour into the baked crust (the crust can be warm or cool).

Using a handheld mixer on high speed, beat the reserved egg whites until soft peaks form. One tablespoon at a time, beat in the remaining ½ cup (4 oz/125 g) plus 2 tablespoons sugar, beating until the egg whites become a meringue with stiff, shiny peaks. Using a spatula, spread the meringue evenly over the hot filling, making sure the meringue touches the crust on all sides (to prevent the meringue from shrinking). Swirl the meringue with the spatula to form peaks. Bake until the meringue is browned, about 5 minutes. Transfer to a rack and cool completely before serving, at least 3 hours.

Cheesecake isn't just a dessert—it is an event. This one is incredibly thick and rich, and also a little bit firm and dense, just as a proper New York—style cheesecake should be. It is at home on both an elegant holiday table and a casual weeknight supper menu. Take care not to overbake it, or it will crack as it cools.

CHERRY CHEESECAKE

Makes 12 servings

Unsalted butter, 4 tablespoons (2 oz/ 60 g), melted, plus more for the pan

Graham cracker crumbs, 1 cup (3 oz/90 g)

Slivered blanched almonds, ½ cup (2½ oz/75 g)

Sugar, 1½ cups (12 oz/375 g) plus 3 tablespoons

Cream cheese, 2 pounds (1 kg), at room temperature

All-purpose flour, 2 tablespoons

Kosher salt

Sour cream, ½ cup (4 oz/125 g)

Pure vanilla extract, 1 tablespoon

Large eggs, 3, at room temperature

Cherries, 1 pound (500 g), pitted and halved

Cherry juice, ½ cup (4 fl oz/125 ml)

Cornstarch, 1 tablespoon

To make the crust, preheat the oven to 350°F (180°C). Butter a 9-inch (23-cm) round springform pan. In a food processor, combine the cracker crumbs, almonds, and the 3 tablespoons sugar and process until finely ground. Drizzle in the butter and pulse until well blended and evenly moistened. Transfer to the prepared pan and press evenly into the bottom and about 1½ inches (4 cm) up the sides. Bake until golden and set, about 7 minutes. Let cool completely on a rack. Reduce the oven temperature to 300°F (150°C).

To make the filling, in a stand mixer fitted with the paddle attachment, combine the cream cheese, flour, and ¼ teaspoon salt. Beat on medium-high speed until smooth, stopping as needed to scrape down the bowl. Add 1¼ cups (10 oz/315 g) of the sugar, the sour cream, and the vanilla and beat until blended, again stopping to scrape down the bowl as needed. Add the eggs, one at a time, beating after each addition. Pour the filling into the cooled crust. Bake the cheesecake until the filling is set but the center still jiggles slightly when the pan is gently shaken, about 1 hour. (The filling will firm as it cools.) Transfer to a wire rack. Carefully run a sharp knife around the inside of the pan to loosen the cheesecake. Let cool to room temperature.

Cover and refrigerate until cold, at least 3 hours.

Meanwhile, make the cherry topping. In a saucepan, combine the cherries, cherry juice, the remaining ¼ cup (2 oz/60 g) sugar, and a pinch of salt and cook over medium-high heat, stirring, until the cherries soften, 2—3 minutes. In a bowl, stir together the cornstarch and 1 tablespoon water, then add to the cherry mixture. Cook just until the liquid comes to a boil and thickens, about 3 minutes. Transfer to a bowl to cool.

To serve, unclasp and remove the pan sides. Slide the cheesecake onto a serving platter. Cut into wedges and serve with the cherry topping on each slice.

Change it up For a lemony cheesecake, add 2 teaspoons grated lemon zest to the filling with the vanilla. Instead of the cherry topping, serve the cheesecake with sliced, sugared strawberries.

Cobblers celebrate ripe, juicy fruit of all kinds. No amount of sugar will improve the flavor of hard, flavorless, out-of-season fruits, so wait until you have the perfect specimens before you make a cobbler. Arguably, peaches make the best cobbler of all, and a scoop of vanilla ice cream makes a good thing even better.

PEACH COBBLER

Makes 8 servings

Unsalted butter, 6 tablespoons (3 oz/90 g), plus more for the baking dish

Peaches, 5 pounds (2.5 kg)

Light brown sugar, ½ cup (3½ oz/105 g) firmly packed

Cornstarch, 2 tablespoons

Half-and-half, ¾ cup (6 fl oz/180 ml)

Large egg, 1

Pure vanilla extract, 1 teaspoon

All-purpose flour, 2 cups (10 oz/315 g)

Granulated sugar, ¼ cup (2 oz/60 g), plus more for sprinkling

Baking powder, 1 tablespoon

Fine sea salt, ½ teaspoon

Preheat the oven to 375°F (190°C). Lightly butter a 9-by-13-inch (23-by-33-cm) baking dish. Have ready a bowl of ice water.

Bring a large pot of water to a boil over high heat. A few at a time, plunge the peaches into the boiling water just until the skins loosen, about 1 minute. Using a slotted spoon, transfer to the bowl of ice water. Peel, pit, and slice the peaches; you should have about 12 cups (72 oz/2.25 kg).

In a bowl, toss together the peaches, brown sugar, and cornstarch. Spread in the prepared baking dish, place the dish on a baking sheet, and bake for 15 minutes.

Meanwhile, in a bowl, whisk together the half-and-half, egg, and vanilla until well blended. In another bowl, sift together the flour, the ¼ cup (2 oz/60 g) granulated sugar, baking powder, and salt. Cut the butter into tablespoons and scatter over the flour mixture. Using a pastry blender or 2 knives, cut the butter into the flour mixture just until the mixture forms coarse crumbs the size of peas. Add the half-and-half mixture and stir just until the dough comes together.

When the filling has baked for 15 minutes, remove it from the oven. Drop the dough onto the filling in 8 heaping, evenly spaced spoonfuls. Return to the oven and bake until the peach juices are bubbling, the topping is golden brown, and a toothpick inserted into the topping comes out clean, 30—40 minutes more.

Transfer to a wire rack and let cool for at least 30 minutes, then serve.

Change it up Make your cobbler with 12 cups of your favorite fruit, adjusting the amount of sugar depending on the tartness of the fruit. Try blueberries, raspberries, and blackberries (don't use strawberries because they lose their color when baked); pitted sour cherries; peeled and pitted plums; or peeled, cored, and sliced apples or pears.

Most people would find it tough to choose a favorite pie, but banana cream pie would surely be on many short lists. Another diner classic that shines even more brightly when made at home, each bite features a heavenly medley of buttery crust, velvety vanilla filling, rich whipped cream, and slices of ripe, sweet banana.

BANANA CREAM PIE

Makes 8 servings

Flour for dusting

Flaky Pastry Dough (page 217)

Whole milk, 3 cups (24 fl oz/750 ml)

Cornstarch, 1/3 cup (1 1/3 oz/40 g)

Large egg yolks, 4

Sugar, 2/3 cup (5 oz/155 g)

Fine sea salt, 1/8 teaspoon

Vanilla bean, 1

Unsalted butter, 2 tablespoons, cut into tablespoons

Bananas, 2 large, peeled and thinly sliced

Whipped Cream (page 217)

Chocolate Curls (page 217), for serving (optional)

Place the unwrapped dough on a floured work surface and dust with flour. (If the dough is cold, let it stand for a few minutes to soften.) Roll out into a round about 12 inches (30 cm) in diameter and 1/8 inch (3 mm) thick. Transfer to a 9-inch (23-cm) pie dish, fitting the dough into the bottom and sides. Trim the dough, leaving a 3/4-inch (2-cm) overhang. Fold the overhang under, then flute the edge. Using a fork, pierce the dough all over, then line with aluminum foil and freeze for 30 minutes. Meanwhile, position a rack in the lower third of the oven and preheat to 375°F (190°C). Place the dough-lined pan on a baking sheet and fill the foil with pie weights. Bake until the dough looks dry and is barely golden, 12–15 minutes. Remove the foil and weights. Continue baking until the crust is golden brown, 12–15 minutes more. Transfer to a rack and cool completely.

In a small bowl, whisk together 1/2 cup (4 fl oz/125 ml) of the milk and the cornstarch. In a heatproof bowl, beat the yolks until blended. Gradually whisk the milk mixture into the yolks.

In a saucepan, combine the remaining 2 1/2 cups (20 fl oz/625 ml) milk, the sugar, and salt. Using a paring knife, slit the vanilla bean in half lengthwise, scrape out the seeds into the saucepan, and add the pod. Place over medium heat and bring to a simmer, stirring to dissolve the sugar. Gradually whisk the hot milk mixture into the egg mixture, then return to the saucepan. Heat over medium heat until the mixture comes to a boil, whisking constantly. Reduce the heat to low and let bubble for 30 seconds. Remove from the heat and whisk in the butter. Strain through a medium-mesh sieve into a stainless-steel bowl to remove any bits of cooked egg white and the vanilla pod. Press a piece of plastic wrap directly onto the surface of the filling, and pierce the plastic a few times with a knife tip to allow the steam to escape. Place the bowl in a larger bowl of ice water and let cool until lukewarm.

Spread the banana slices in the cooled pie crust. Spread the filling on top. Press a clean piece of plastic wrap directly on the surface of the filling and refrigerate until chilled, at least 1 hour. Remove the plastic wrap. Spread and swirl the whipped cream over the filling. Refrigerate until ready to serve. When ready to serve, scatter the chocolate curls, if using, over the whipped cream topping, and serve in wedges.

There is nothing more homey, autumnal, and American than a warm apple pie cooling on the kitchen counter. Look for good baking apples, such as Mutsu, Pink Lady, or Empire, for making this traditional dessert, then top each slice with a scoop of vanilla ice cream or slices of sharp Cheddar cheese to stay with tradition.

APPLE PIE

Makes 8 servings

Baking apples,
3 pounds (1.5 kg)

Light brown sugar,
⅓ cup (2½ oz/75 g)
firmly packed

Granulated sugar,
⅓ cup (3 oz/90 g)

Fresh lemon juice,
2 tablespoons

All-purpose flour,
2 tablespoons, plus
more for dusting

Ground cinnamon,
½ teaspoon

**Double recipe of
Flaky Pastry Dough
(page 217)**

Unsalted butter,
2 tablespoons,
thinly sliced

Egg yolk, 1

Heavy cream,
1 tablespoon

Position a rack in the bottom third of the oven and preheat to 400°F (200°C). Peel and core the apples and cut into thin wedges. In a large bowl, toss together the apples, both sugars, lemon juice, flour, and cinnamon. Set aside.

Place the unwrapped dough on a lightly floured work surface and divide in half. Rewrap one half of the dough and set aside. (If the dough is chilled hard, let it stand at room temperature for a few minutes until it begins to soften before rolling it out.)

Dust the top of the dough with flour and roll out into a round about 12 inches (30 cm) in diameter and ⅛ inch (3 mm) thick. Transfer to a 9-inch (23-cm) pie dish, gently fitting the dough into the bottom and sides of the dish. Using scissors or a small knife, trim the dough, leaving a ¾-inch (2-cm) overhang. Reserve the trimmings to decorate the top crust. Spread the apple mixture in the pie dish and scatter the butter slices on top.

Place the second half of the dough on a lightly floured work surface and dust the top with flour. Roll out into a round about 12 inches (30 cm) in diameter and ⅛ inch (3 mm) thick. Center the round over the apple filling. Trim the dough so it is even with the bottom crust, reserving the excess pastry. Fold the overhang under so the dough is flush with the pan rim, then press together to seal. Flute the edge decoratively, if desired. Cut a few slits in the top crust for steam to escape.

In a small bowl, whisk the egg yolk and cream together to make a glaze. Lightly brush the top crust with some of the glaze. Roll out the reserved pastry scraps to a thickness of ⅛-inch (3mm). Using a small sharp knife, cut out leaf shapes for decoration. Use the dull side of the knife to make vein markings on the leaves. Arrange the leaves decoratively on the pastry, and brush again with the egg wash. Refrigerate the pie for 15 minutes.

Place the pie dish on a rimmed baking sheet. Bake for 15 minutes. Reduce the oven temperature to 350°F (180°C) and continue baking until the crust is golden brown and the juices visible through the slits are bubbling, about 1 hour. Transfer to a wire rack to cool. Serve warm or at room temperature.

Even though strawberries are available year-round in supermarkets, you should wait to make this recipe until your local crop comes into season in the spring. Your patience will be rewarded with juicy berries that sing with flavor and take this beloved classic over the top. And don't be shy with the whipped cream.

STRAWBERRY SHORTCAKES

Makes 6 servings

Strawberries, 1½ pounds (750 g), hulled and sliced

Sugar, 6 tablespoons (3 oz/90 g)

All-purpose flour, 2 cups (10 oz/315 g)

Baking powder, 1 tablespoon

Fine sea salt, ¼ teaspoon

Unsalted butter, 6 tablespoons (3 oz/90 g)

Heavy cream, 1 cup (8 fl oz/250 ml)

Whipped Cream (page 217)

In a bowl, toss the strawberries with 3 tablespoons of the sugar. Cover and refrigerate until the berries release their juices, at least 2 hours or up to 6 hours.

Preheat the oven to 400°F (200°C). Have ready an ungreased rimmed baking sheet.

In a bowl, sift together the flour, the remaining 3 tablespoons sugar, the baking powder, and the salt. Cut the butter into tablespoons and scatter over the flour mixture. Using a pastry blender or 2 knives, cut the butter into the flour mixture just until the mixture forms coarse crumbs the size of peas. Add the cream and stir just until the dough comes together.

Turn out the dough onto a lightly floured work surface and knead gently just until smooth. Using a light touch, pat out the dough into a round about ½ inch (12 mm) thick. Using a 3-inch (7.5-cm) round biscuit or cookie cutter, cut out as many dough rounds as possible and place them 1 inch (2.5 cm) apart on the baking sheet. Gather up the scraps, pat them out again, and cut out more dough rounds to make a total of 6 shortcakes. Add them to the baking sheet.

Bake the shortcakes until golden brown, 15–18 minutes. Let cool on the baking sheet on a wire rack until warm.

To serve, split each shortcake in half horizontally and place a shortcake bottom, cut side up, on a dessert plate. Top each shortcake bottom with a heaping spoonful of strawberries with their juices and a dollop of whipped cream. Place the shortcake top over the whipped cream and serve at once.

Change it up Blackberries, blueberries, raspberries, nectarines, and peaches (or a combination) all go great with shortcake. For a grown-up variation, substitute ¼ cup (2 fl oz/60 ml) orange-flavored liqueur, such as Grand Marnier, for the sugar, then add a little sugar to taste, if you wish.

Eating a cupcake brings out the kid in all of us. It's like having your very own little cake that you don't have to share with anyone. Topped with a thick layer of luscious cream cheese frosting and sprinkled with toasted coconut, these coconut cupcakes have a tender, moist crumb that literally melts in your mouth.

COCONUT CUPCAKES

Makes 12 cupcakes

All-purpose flour, 1¾ cups (9 oz/280 g)

Baking powder, 2 teaspoons

Fine sea salt, ¼ teaspoon

Granulated sugar, 1 cup (8 oz/250 g)

Unsalted butter, ½ cup (4 oz/125 g), at room temperature

Large eggs, 3, separated

Vanilla extract, 1 teaspoon

Coconut milk, ½ cup (4 fl oz/125 ml)

Sweetened dried coconut flakes, 1 cup (4 oz/120 g)

CREAM CHEESE FROSTING

Sweetened dried coconut flakes, ½ cup (2 oz/60 g)

Cream cheese, 6 ounces (185 g), at room temperature

Unsalted butter, 4 tablespoons (2 oz/60 g), at room temperature

Lemon juice, 2 teaspoons

Vanilla extract, ½ teaspoon

Confectioners' sugar, 3 cups (12 oz/375 g), sifted

To make the cupcakes, preheat the oven to 350°F (180°C). Line 12 muffin cups with paper liners. In a bowl, sift together the flour, baking powder, and salt. In another bowl, using a handheld mixer on medium-high speed, beat together the sugar and butter until the mixture is light in texture, 2–3 minutes. Beat in the egg yolks, one at a time, then beat in the vanilla. Reduce the speed to low and add the flour mixture in 3 additions alternately with the coconut milk in 2 additions, beginning and ending with the flour mixture and scraping down the bowl as needed, beating just until smooth.

In another bowl, using the mixer on high speed, beat the egg whites until soft peaks form. Stir one-fourth of the whites into the batter to lighten it, then fold in the remaining whites, leaving some whites visible. Gently fold in the coconut flakes. Divide the batter evenly among the lined muffin cups, filling them about three-fourths full. Bake until a toothpick inserted in the center of a cupcake comes out clean, about 20 minutes. Let cool for 5 minutes in the pan, then turn out of the pan onto a wire rack and let cool completely. Leave the oven on.

To make the frosting, spread the coconut flakes on a rimmed baking sheet. Bake, stirring occasionally, until lightly toasted, about 10 minutes. Let cool completely. In a bowl, using the mixer on low speed, beat together the cream cheese, butter, lemon juice, and vanilla. Gradually beat in the confectioners' sugar until the icing is smooth. Spread the frosting on the cooled cupcakes, dividing it equally. Sprinkle with the toasted coconut, then serve.

Change it up For coconut layer cake, divide the batter between 2 buttered and floured 8-inch (20-cm) round cake pans. Bake until the cakes begin to pull away from the sides of the pans, about 25 minutes. Make a double batch of the frosting and assemble the cake as directed for Devil's Food Layer Cake (page 197). Garnish with 1 cup (3 oz/90 g) toasted dried coconut flakes.

If to you, baking brownies has meant using the recipe on the back of a brownie-mix box or can of cocoa powder, you are in for a treat. These thick, chewy, deeply chocolate brownies are dark, rich, and irresistible; not to mention, they require little more effort than the inferior boxed version.

DARK CHOCOLATE BROWNIES

Makes 20 brownies

Unsalted butter, ¾ cup (6 oz/185 g), plus more for the baking pan

All-purpose flour, 1 cup (5 oz/155 g), plus more for dusting

Baking soda, ½ teaspoon

Fine sea salt, ½ teaspoon

Unsweetened chocolate, 6 ounces (185 g), finely chopped

Granulated sugar, 1 cup (8 oz/250 g)

Light brown sugar, 1 cup (7 oz/220 g) firmly packed

Large eggs, 4, at room temperature

Light corn syrup, honey, or maple syrup, ¼ cup (3 fl oz/80 g)

Pure vanilla extract, 2 teaspoons

Semisweet or bittersweet chocolate chips, 1 cup (6 oz/185 g)

Preheat the oven to 350°F (180°C). Butter a 9-by-13-inch (23-by-33-cm) baking pan. Press a 20-inch (50-cm) length of parchment paper into the bottom and up the sides of the pan, folding the parchment as needed to fit and allowing the excess to hang over the sides. Lightly butter the parchment and dust with flour, tapping out the excess.

In a bowl, sift together the flour, baking soda, and salt. In a saucepan, melt the butter over medium heat. Remove from the heat and add the unsweetened chocolate. Let stand for 3 minutes, then whisk until smooth. Whisk in both the sugars until well blended. Whisk in the eggs, one at a time, then whisk in the corn syrup and vanilla until blended. Add the flour mixture and stir with a wooden spoon until combined. Stir in the chocolate chips, distributing them evenly. Spread the batter in the prepared pan and smooth the top.

Bake until a toothpick inserted into the center comes out with a few moist crumbs attached, about 25 minutes. Let cool completely in the pan on a wire rack. Run a knife around the inside of the pan to release the sides of the brownie. Lift up the whole brownie by the parchment "handles" and remove it from the pan.

Cut the brownie into 20 squares and serve. Leftovers can be stored in an airtight container at room temperature for up to 3 days.

Change it up If you think that brownies must have nuts, add 1 cup (4 oz/125 g) coarsely chopped toasted walnuts to the batter instead of the chocolate chips. For an outrageous brownie sundae, top a brownie with a big scoop of your favorite ice cream, drizzle with Hot Fudge Sauce (page 201), and crown with a big dollop of Whipped Cream (page 217).

There are chocolate chip cookies, and then there are these chocolate chip cookies: large, chewy, buttery, and with just the right amount of chips and nuts. Choose good-quality chocolate for the tastiest result.

CHOCOLATE CHIP COOKIES

Makes about 3 dozen cookies

Walnut pieces, 1 cup (4 oz/125 g)

All-purpose flour, 2¼ cups (11½ oz/360 g)

Baking soda, 1 teaspoon

Kosher salt, 1 teaspoon

Unsalted butter, 1 cup (8 oz/250 g), at room temperature

Granulated sugar, ⅔ cup (5 oz/155 g)

Light brown sugar, ⅔ cup (5 oz/155 g) firmly packed

Large eggs, 1 whole plus 1 yolk

Light corn syrup, honey, or maple syrup, 2 tablespoons

Pure vanilla extract, 2 teaspoons

Semisweet chocolate, 12 ounces (375 g), chopped into ½-inch (12-mm) chunks

Preheat the oven to 350°F (180°C). Spread the walnuts in a single layer on a rimmed baking sheet. Place in the oven and toast, stirring occasionally, until they are fragrant and toasted, about 10 minutes. Let cool, then coarsely chop.

In a bowl, sift together the flour, baking soda, and salt. In another bowl, using a handheld mixer on medium-high speed, beat together the butter and both the sugars until the mixture is light in texture, about 3 minutes. Beat in the whole egg and egg yolk, then the corn syrup and vanilla. Reduce the speed to low and gradually add the flour mixture, beating just until smooth and stopping to scrape down the bowl as needed. With a spoon, stir in the chopped chocolate and chopped walnuts, distributing them evenly throughout the dough. Cover and refrigerate until cold, at least 2 hours or up to 6 hours.

Position racks in the center and upper third of the oven and preheat to 350°F (180°C). Line 2 rimmed baking sheets with parchment paper. Drop rounded tablespoonfuls of the chilled dough onto the baking sheets, spacing them about 1 inch (2.5 cm) apart.

Place 1 sheet on each oven rack and bake, switching the pans between the racks and rotating them 180 degrees halfway through baking, until the cookies are lightly browned, 8–10 minutes. Let cool for 3 minutes on the baking sheets, then transfer to wire racks to cool slightly before serving. These cookies can be stored in an airtight container for up to 5 days.

Change it up If you want to make milk or white chocolate chip cookies, use chips rather than bar chocolate because they hold their shape better when baked. You can also make cookies with a mixture of semisweet, white, and milk chips. Try pecans, almonds, or peanuts in place of the walnuts.

No one can resist a thick slice of freshly baked banana bread, especially when studded with melting chocolate chips and toasty walnuts. Baking this bread is a good way to take advantage of fruit that has been languishing on the counter throughout the busy week. The riper the bananas, the sweeter the bread will be.

WALNUT-CHOCOLATE CHIP BANANA BREAD

Makes 1 loaf

Unsalted butter, 6 tablespoons (3 oz/90 g), at room temperature, plus more for the loaf pan

All-purpose flour, 2 cups (10 oz/315 g), plus more for dusting

Bananas, 3 very ripe, peeled

Baking soda, 1 teaspoon

Fine sea salt, ¼ teaspoon

Sugar, ¾ cup (6 oz/185 g)

Eggs, 2 large, beaten

Sour cream, ½ cup (4 oz/125 g), at room temperature

Semisweet chocolate chips, 1 cup (6 oz/185 g)

Walnuts, 1 cup (4 oz/125 g) coarsely chopped, toasted

Preheat the oven to 350°F (180°C). Lightly butter a 9-by-5-inch (23-by-13-cm) loaf pan. Line the bottom and long sides of the pan with parchment paper. Butter the top of the parchment. Dust the pan with flour, tapping out the excess.

Using a fork, mash the bananas in a bowl; you should have about 1 cup (8 oz/250 g).

In another bowl, sift together the flour, baking soda, and salt.

In a third bowl, using a handheld mixer on high speed, beat together the butter and sugar until light in color and texture, about 3 minutes. Gradually beat in the eggs and then the mashed bananas. Reduce the speed to low and add the flour mixture in 3 additions alternately with the sour cream in 2 additions, beginning and ending with the flour mixture and stopping to scrape down the bowl as needed, beating until smooth. Fold in the chocolate chips and half of the walnuts. Pour the batter into the prepared pan and smooth the top. Sprinkle the remaining walnuts on top.

Bake until a toothpick inserted in the center comes out clean, about 1 hour. Transfer to a wire rack and let cool in the pan for 5 minutes. Turn out onto the rack and remove the paper. Invert again, and let cool completely. Cut into slices and serve warm or at room temperature.

The secret behind this moist, rich chocolate cake is mixing the cocoa powder—use natural, not Dutch process—with boiling water, which allows the chocolate flavor to blossom and adds extra moisture to the crumb. This time-honored favorite, layered with velvety chocolate frosting, makes the ultimate birthday cake.

DEVIL'S FOOD LAYER CAKE

Makes 10 servings

Unsalted butter,
½ cup (4 oz/125 g)
plus 2 tablespoons, plus
more for greasing,
at room temperature

All-purpose flour,
1¾ cups (9 oz/280 g),
plus more for dusting

Boiling water, 1 cup
(8 fl oz/250 ml)

**Unsweetened natural
cocoa powder,** ¾ cup
(2¼ oz/65 g)

Baking soda,
1½ teaspoons

Fine sea salt, ¼ teaspoon

Sugar, 2 cups (1 lb/500 g)

Large eggs, 3

Pure vanilla extract,
1 teaspoon

Buttermilk, 1¼ cups
(10 fl oz/310 ml)

**Chocolate Frosting
(page 217)**

**Chocolate Curls
(page 217) (optional)**

To make the cake, preheat the oven to 350°F (180°C). Lightly butter two 9-inch (23-cm) round cake pans. Line the bottom of each pan with a round of parchment paper. Dust the pans with flour, tapping out the excess.

In a small heatproof bowl, whisk together the boiling water and cocoa until smooth. Let cool completely. In a bowl, sift together the flour, baking soda, and salt. In a large bowl, using a handheld mixer on medium-high speed, beat together the sugar and butter until the mixture is light in color and texture, about 3 minutes. Beat in the eggs, one at a time, then beat in the vanilla and the cooled cocoa mixture. Reduce the speed to low and add the flour mixture in 3 additions alternately with the buttermilk in 2 additions, beginning and ending with the flour mixture and stopping to scrape down the bowl as needed, beating until smooth. Divide the batter evenly between the prepared pans and smooth the tops. Bake the cakes until they begin to pull away from the sides of the pans, 35—40 minutes. Transfer to wire racks and let cool in the pans for 15 minutes. Run a knife around the inside of each pan to release the cake. Invert the pans onto the racks, lift off the pans, and peel off the parchment paper. Turn each cake right side up and let cool completely.

Make the frosting.

Place 1 cake layer, bottom side up, on a cake plate. Using an icing spatula, spread the top of the layer with a generous ½ cup (4 oz/125 g) of the frosting. Place the second layer, top side down, on top of the first layer. Frost the top, then the sides, with the remaining frosting. Top with chocolate curls, if using. Slice the cake into thick wedges and serve.

Change it up For chocolate cupcakes, line 24 muffin cups with paper liners. Spoon the batter into the prepared cups. Bake until the tops spring back when pressed in the center, 20—25 minutes. Let cool before frosting.

When you make this classic of country cooking, your kitchen will be filled with the heart-warming aroma of simmering apples with cinnamon. Try to make this in the fall, with juicy seasonal apples, because stored apples may be drier and need the extra moisture provided by the optional apple juice.

APPLE & GRANOLA CRISP

Makes 6 servings

Old-fashioned (rolled) oats, 2 cups (6 oz/180 g)

Pecans, 1 cup (4 oz/ 120 g), coarsely chopped

Raisins, 1 cup (6 oz/185 g)

Unsalted butter, 5 tablespoons (2½ oz/ 75 g), plus more for the baking dish

Honey, ¼ cup (3 oz/90 g)

Pure vanilla extract, 1 teaspoon

Ground cinnamon, 1 teaspoon

Baking apples, 4 pounds (2 kg), peeled, cored, and cubed

Light brown sugar, ½ cup (3½ oz/105 g) packed

Fresh lemon juice, 2 tablespoons

Cornstarch, 1 tablespoon

Apple juice or water, ½ cup (4 fl oz/125 ml) (optional)

Vanilla ice cream for serving

Preheat the oven to 350°F (180°C). In a large bowl, mix the oats, pecans, and raisins. In a small saucepan, melt 3 tablespoons of the butter over low heat. Remove from the heat, add the honey, vanilla and ½ teaspoon of the cinnamon, and stir well. Pour the honey mixture over the oat mixture and mix well. Spread evenly on a large rimmed baking sheet.

Bake, stirring often to bring the granola around the edges into the center, until the granola is toasted, about 20 minutes. Let cool.

Lightly butter a (9-by-13-inch) (23-by-33-cm) 3-quart (3-l) baking dish. Thinly slice the remaining 2 tablespoons butter. In a large bowl, toss the apples, brown sugar, sliced butter, lemon juice, cornstarch, and the remaining cinnamon to coat the apples well. Stir in the apple juice, if using. Spread in the baking dish.

Bake, stirring occasionally, until the juices are beginning to bubble around the edges of the pan, about 30 minutes. Sprinkle the granola evenly over the apple mixture and continue baking until the juices are bubbling throughout and the apples are tender, about 15 minutes more. Let cool until warm, about 30 minutes. Serve warm, with the ice cream.

Change it up Although nothing beats homemade granola, you can substitute 3 cups (18 oz/540 g) purchased granola for the freshly baked. Pears make a fine substitute for the apples. You and also add 1 cup (6 oz/185 g) fresh or frozen cranberries to the apples, and increase the brown sugar to ⅔ cup (5 oz/155 g) to sweeten the tart berries.

Going to the ice cream parlor as a kid, banana splits always seemed like the ultimate decadence. But this version—with caramelized bananas, buttery toasted almonds, warm fudge sauce, and fresh cherries—is not your average banana split. Buy the best ice cream your budget allows, or, better yet, make your own.

THE ULTIMATE BANANA SPLIT

Makes 4 servings

HOT FUDGE SAUCE

Heavy cream, ¾ cup (6 fl oz/180 ml)

Light corn syrup, 2 tablespoons

Semisweet chocolate, 6 ounces (185 g), finely chopped

Pure vanilla extract, ½ teaspoon

Slivered blanched almonds, ½ cup (2½ oz/75 g)

Unsalted butter, 1 tablespoon, melted

Kosher salt, ½ teaspoon

Bananas, 4, firm and ripe

Sugar, 8 teaspoons

Vanilla ice cream, about ½ gallon

Whipped cream (page 217)

Cherries with stems, 4

Preheat the oven to 350°F (180°C). To make the hot fudge sauce, in a small saucepan, combine the cream and corn syrup and bring to a simmer over medium heat. Remove from the heat and add the chopped chocolate. Let stand for 3 minutes, then add the vanilla and whisk until smooth. Let cool to lukewarm.

Meanwhile, on a small rimmed baking sheet, toss together the almonds and butter, then spread in a single layer. Place in the oven and toast, stirring occasionally, until golden, about 10 minutes. Remove from the oven and sprinkle with the salt. Let cool on the baking sheet.

Halve the unpeeled bananas lengthwise. Sprinkle the cut sides of each banana half with 1 teaspoon sugar. Heat a large nonstick frying pan over medium heat.

In batches to avoid crowding, add the banana halves, cut sides down, and cook just until the sugar is caramelized, about 30 seconds. Transfer to a plate.

To make each banana split, peel 2 banana halves and arrange, caramelized sides up, in a banana-split dish or an oblong bowl. Place 3 scoops of ice cream between the banana halves. Top with the hot fudge sauce, a sprinkle of the toasted almonds, and a large dollop of whipped cream. Perch a cherry on top and serve at once.

Change it up

Many ice cream parlors make their banana splits with a scoop each of vanilla, strawberry, and chocolate, and you may wish to follow suit. Or, use your favorite flavor of ice cream. You can also substitute toasted peanuts or cashews for the almonds.

In the past, most home cooks made pineapple upside-down cake with canned pineapple and enough brown sugar to set your teeth on edge. Nowadays, you can pick up a fresh pineapple in most markets and reduce the amount of topping to suit contemporary tastes. Be brave when inverting the cake—it's not that difficult.

PINEAPPLE UPSIDE-DOWN CAKE

Makes 8 servings

Pineapple, 1

Light brown sugar, 1 cup
(7 oz/220 g) firmly packed

Unsalted butter,
6 tablespoons (3 oz/90 g),
plus ½ cup (4 oz/125 g)
at room temperature

All-purpose flour,
1½ cups (7 12 oz/235 g)

Baking powder,
1½ teaspoons

Fine sea salt, ¼ teaspoon

Granulated sugar,
1 cup (8 oz/250 g)

Large eggs, 2, at
room temperature

Pure vanilla extract,
1 teaspoon

Whole milk, ½ cup
(4 fl oz/125 ml)

Preheat the oven to 350°F (180°C). Cut off the crown and stem end of the pineapple. Holding the pineapple upright, pare off the skin, removing as little of the flesh as possible. With the pineapple on its side, cut shallow furrows to remove all of the brown "eyes." Cut the pineapple lengthwise into quarters, then trim away the fibrous core. Cut the fruit into chunks and set aside. You should have 2 cups (12 oz/370 g).

In a 10-inch (25-cm) cast-iron frying pan, combine the brown sugar and the 6 tablespoons (3 oz/90 g) butter and heat over medium heat, stirring frequently, until the butter is melted and the mixture is bubbling. Spread the pineapple chunks evenly in the pan. Set aside. In a bowl, sift together the flour, baking powder, and salt. In another bowl, using a handheld mixer on medium-high speed, beat together the granulated sugar and the ½ cup (4 oz/125 g) butter until the mixture is light in color and texture, about 3 minutes.

Beat in the eggs, one at a time, then beat in the vanilla. Reduce the speed to low and add the flour mixture in 3 additions alternately with the milk in 2 additions, beginning and ending with the flour mixture and stopping to scrape down the bowl as needed, beating until smooth. Spread the batter evenly over the pineapple.

Bake the cake until golden brown and a toothpick inserted in the center comes out clean, about 35 minutes. Let cool in the pan on a wire rack for 5 minutes.

Run a knife around the inside of the pan to release the cake. Invert a platter or cake plate over the pan. Holding the platter and pan together, invert them and give them a good shake to unmold the cake. Lift off the pan. Let cool until warm, then serve.

Change it up Scatter ½ cup (2 oz/60 g) chopped pecans over the butter and brown sugar mixture in the frying pan just before adding the pineapple. You can also substitute 2 cups (12 oz/370 g) peeled, pitted, and sliced peaches or peeled, cored, and sliced apples or pears for the pineapple.

Here's how to make a creamy, rich rice pudding guaranteed to make any cook proud. Starchy Italian rice used for making risotto, such as Arborio or Carnaroli, helps thicken this pudding without eggs. The recipe requires your patience and attention as it bakes, so make it on a day when you have time on your hands.

BAKED RICE PUDDING

Makes 4-6 servings

Unsalted butter, 1 tablespoon, plus more for the baking dish

Whole milk, 4 cups (32 fl oz/1 l), or as needed

Arborio or Carnaroli rice, ⅓ cup (2⅓ oz/75 g)

Sugar, ⅓ cup (3 oz/90 g)

Cinnamon stick, ½

Pure vanilla extract, 1 teaspoon

Finely grated orange zest, from 1 orange

Fine sea salt

Whipped Cream (page 217)

Preheat the oven to 300°F (150°C). Lightly butter a shallow 2-quart (2-l) baking dish. In a saucepan, combine the 4 cups (32 fl oz/1 l) milk, the rice, sugar, butter, and cinnamon stick and bring to a simmer over medium heat, stirring to dissolve the sugar. Pour into the prepared baking dish and distribute the rice evenly. Bake, stirring with a wooden spoon every 15—20 minutes, until the rice is very tender and has absorbed most of the milk, about 1½ hours.

Remove from the oven and stir in the vanilla, orange zest, and a pinch of salt. If the pudding seems too thick, stir in milk until it is the consistency you desire. Serve warm, or let cool to room temperature, cover, and refrigerate until chilled. Spoon into bowls, top with whipped cream, and serve.

Change it up While some remember picking the raisins out of our rice pudding, others can't imagine rice pudding without dried fruit. If you wish, add ½ cup (3 oz/90 g) raisins or dried currants, cherries, cranberries, blueberries, or chopped figs, stirring them into the pudding with the vanilla.

When peaches are at their seasonal peak, there is comfort in knowing that they can speak for themselves with only a few added flavorings. In this simple recipe, they are roasted with honey to bring out their juices, and served with a dollop of creamy mascarpone as a simple dessert, and maybe a butter cookie or two.

HONEY-GLAZED ROASTED PEACHES WITH MASCARPONE

Makes 4-6 servings

Mascarpone cheese, ½ cup (4 oz/125 g)

Heavy cream, 3 tablespoons

Ground cinnamon, ¼ teaspoon (optional)

Butter, 2 tablespoons melted

Peaches, 4 ripe, preferably freestone, pitted and halved lengthwise

Honey, 2 tablespoons, slightly warmed until liquid

Fresh thyme, a few sprigs (optional), for garnish

Preheat the oven to 400°F (200°C). In a small bowl, mix together the mascarpone, cream, and cinnamon, if using, with a rubber spatula. Set aside and let stand at room temperature while roasting the peaches.

Have ready a baking dish just large enough to hold the peach halves in a single layer. Butter the dish with 1 tablespoon of the melted butter. Place the peaches in the dish, cut side up, and brush the halves with the remaining 1 tablespoon melted butter.

Bake until the peach juices collect in the hollows where the pits were removed, about 15 minutes. Remove from the oven. Brush the peaches with the honey, letting the juices run into the baking dish. Return to the oven and bake until the peaches are tender, about 5 minutes more. Serve the peaches at once, with the cooking juices spooned on top, and top with the mascarpone and thyme, if using.

Change it up Grill the buttered peach halves over medium heat for 5 minutes, then brush them with the warm honey and grill until tender, about 2 minutes more.

Even at its simplest, bread pudding is scrumptious. Using challah or another egg bread, such as brioche or panettone, gives this version extra richness and substance, and then two things take it over the top: caramelized sugar, which adds incredible depth of flavor, and a scattering of bright red raspberries to finish.

MAPLE BREAD PUDDING

Makes 8 servings

Challah, 1 loaf (about 1 pound/500 g)

Whole milk, 4 cups (32 fl oz/1 l)

Unsalted butter, ½ cup (4 oz/125 g), plus more for the baking dish

Fine sea salt

Sugar, 1⅔ cups (13 oz/410 g)

Light corn syrup, 1 tablespoon

Large eggs, 5

Pure maple extract, 1 teaspoon

Pure vanilla extract, 1 teaspoons

Pure maple syrup, ⅔ cup (3⅔ oz/115 g)

Brandy, ¼ cup (2 fl oz/60 ml)

Raspberries, 4 cups (16 oz/500 g)

Whipped Cream (page 217) or crème fraîche for serving

Confectioners' (powdered) sugar for serving

Preheat the oven to 350°F (180°C). Cut the challah into ¾-inch (2-cm) slices. Alternatively, cut the bread into 1-inch (2.5-cm) cubes. You will have about 8 cups (16 oz/480 g). Spread the bread slices on 1 or 2 rimmed baking sheets. Bake until the bread is dry around the edges but not toasted, 10–12 minutes. Let cool. Reduce the oven temperature to 300°F (150°C).

In a saucepan, heat the milk, butter, and a pinch of salt over medium heat, stirring frequently, until the butter is melted. Set aside and cover. In a large saucepan, combine the sugar, corn syrup, and ¼ cup (2 fl oz/60 ml) water and stir to moisten the sugar. Place over high heat and bring to a boil, stirring constantly. Stop stirring and cook, brushing down any crystals that form on the sides of the pan with a pastry brush dipped in cold water and occasionally swirling the saucepan by its handle, until the sugar turns a deep golden brown caramel. The caramel will have a toasty aroma, and you may see some wisps of smoke. Reduce the heat to low. Gradually and very carefully stir the warm milk mixture into the caramel; the mixture will boil furiously. Cook, stirring constantly, until the mixture is smooth and the caramel is completely dissolved. Remove from the heat.

Lightly butter a 3-quart (3-l) baking dish. Arrange 2 layers of the bread slices in the dish, tearing the slices as needed to fill in any spaces. In a very large heatproof bowl, whisk the eggs until blended. Gradually whisk in the caramel mixture, then the maple and vanilla extracts. Gradually pour over the bread slices, pressing down with a spatula to saturate the bread evenly. Let stand for 15 minutes.

Place the dish in a large roasting pan. Place the roasting pan in the oven and add hot water to the pan to come halfway up the sides of the baking dish. Bake until a knife inserted in the center of the pudding comes out clean, about 40 minutes. Transfer to a wire rack and let cool for 10 minutes.

To make the brandied maple sauce, combine the maple syrup and brandy in a small saucepan. Bring to a boil over medium heat, then reduce the heat to low and simmer 2 minutes. Let cool slightly, and transfer to a small pitcher. Serve the pudding in bowls, scattered with the raspberries, with a dollop of whipped cream on each serving. Sprinkle lightly with confectioners' sugar and pass the warm brandied maple sauce at the table.

Spoon for spoon, is there any dessert more comforting than pudding? Of the trio of vanilla, chocolate, and butterscotch flavors, the last one arguably has the most dedicated fans. But many people have tasted only the boxed kind. Here is the real deal, infused with caramel and the rich flavor of butter.

REAL BUTTERSCOTCH PUDDING

Makes 4-6 servings

Large egg yolks, 6

Cornstarch, ⅓ cup (1¾ oz/50 g) plus 1 tablespoon

Whole milk, 3 cups (24 fl oz/750 ml)

Unsalted butter, 6 tablespoons (3 oz/90 g)

Fine sea salt

Sugar, 1¼ cups (10 oz/315 g)

Pure vanilla extract, 1 teaspoon

Whipped Cream (page 217)

In a heatproof bowl, whisk together the egg yolks, cornstarch, and ½ cup (4 fl oz/125 ml) of the milk until well blended. In a small saucepan, combine the remaining 2½ cups (20 fl oz/625 ml) milk, the butter, and a pinch of salt and heat over medium heat, stirring frequently, until the butter is melted. Set aside and cover to keep warm.

In a large saucepan, combine the sugar and ¼ cup (2 fl oz/60 ml) water and stir to moisten the sugar. Place over high heat and bring to a boil, stirring constantly. Stop stirring and cook, brushing down any crystals that form on the inside of the pan with a pastry brush dipped in cold water and occasionally swirling the saucepan by its handle, until the sugar turns a deep golden brown caramel. The caramel will have a toasty aroma, and you may see some wisps of smoke. Reduce the heat to low. Gradually and very carefully stir the warm milk mixture into the caramel; the mixture will boil furiously. Cook, stirring constantly, until the mixture is smooth and the caramel is completely dissolved. Gradually whisk the hot caramel mixture into the egg mixture.

Return to the saucepan and heat over medium heat until the mixture comes to a full boil, whisking constantly. Strain through a coarse-mesh sieve placed over a bowl. Stir in the vanilla. Press a piece of plastic wrap directly onto the surface of the pudding, and pierce the plastic a few times with a knife tip to allow the steam to escape.

Let cool to lukewarm, then refrigerate until cold, about 2 hours. Layer the chilled pudding and whipped cream evenly in 4—6 parfait glasses or footed bowls. Serve at once, or chill for up to 8 hours before serving.

Change it up For a top-notch banana pudding, in individual bowls, layer the butterscotch pudding with sliced bananas, vanilla wafers, and whipped cream. Chill for a couple of hours to soften the cookies.

Malted milk powder—just 2 simple tablespoons—transforms a vanilla milkshake into an irresistible dessert, appreciated by all old-school palettes. This timeless take on the milkshake imparts a slightly toasty flavor from the evaporated milk.

VANILLA MALTEDS

Makes 2 servings

Whole milk, ⅓ cup (3 fl oz/80 ml), or as needed

Pure vanilla extract, 1 teaspoon

Malted milk powder, 2 tablespoons

Vanilla bean ice cream, 2½ cups (17½ oz/550 g)

Whipped Cream (page 217)

In the following order, put the ⅓ cup (3 fl oz/80 ml) milk, vanilla extract, malted milk powder, and ice cream in a blender. Cover and process until smooth, adding more milk if necessary to achieve the consistency you desire.

Pour into 2 tall, chilled glasses, top each with a dollop of whipped cream, add a tall straw, and serve at once.

Change it up You can easily turn this into a chocolate malted. Instead of the vanilla bean ice cream, use chocolate ice cream or your favorite premium-quality chocolate ice cream.

BASIC RECIPES

CHICKEN STOCK

Whole chicken with giblets, 1 (about 4 pounds/2 kg)

Yellow onion, 1, coarsely chopped

Carrot, 1 large, coarsely chopped

Celery, 1 large stalk, coarsely chopped

Fresh flat-leaf parsley, 4 sprigs

Fresh thyme, 4 sprigs, or ½ teaspoon dried

Black peppercorns, ¼ teaspoon

Bay leaf, 1

MAKES ABOUT 2 QUARTS (2 L)

Pull the fat from the chicken cavity, chop, and set aside. Using a large knife, cut the chicken into 2 wings, 2 breast halves, 2 drumsticks, 2 thighs, and the back. Reserve the heart, gizzard, kidneys, and liver for another use.

In a stockpot, heat the chopped fat over medium-low heat until it melts. Add the onion, carrot, and celery and raise the heat to medium. Cover and cook, stirring occasionally, until the vegetables soften, about 5 minutes.

Uncover and add the cut-up chicken, the giblets, and cold water to cover by 1 inch (2.5 cm) (about 3 quarts/3 l). Raise the heat to high and bring to a boil, skimming off any foam that rises to the surface. Add the parsley, thyme, peppercorns, and bay leaf, reduce the heat to low, and simmer gently, uncovered, until the chicken breasts show no sign of pink when pierced with a knife in the thickest part, about 45 minutes.

Remove the breasts from the pot, leaving the rest of the parts simmering in the stock. Remove the skin and bones from the breasts and return them to the pot. Set the breast meat aside. Continue simmering the stock until full-flavored, about 30 minutes more.

Remove the stock from the heat and strain through a colander set over a large heatproof bowl. Remove the thighs and drumsticks from the colander. Discard their skin and bones along with the solids in the colander. Add the meat from the drumsticks and thighs to the reserved breast meat. Let cool, cover, and refrigerate for use in soup or another recipe.

Let the stock stand for 5 minutes, then skim off the fat from the surface. Use at once, or let cool, cover, and refrigerate for up to 3 days or freeze for up to 3 months.

BEEF STOCK

Meaty beef bones, such as shank, neck, or ribs (1½ pounds/750 g)

Canola oil, 1 tablespoon

Yellow onion, 1, coarsely chopped

Carrot, 1, coarsely chopped

Celery, 1 stalk with leaves, chopped

Fresh flat-leaf parsley, 8 sprigs

Fresh thyme, 6 sprigs, or ½ teaspoon dried

Black peppercorns, ¼ teaspoon

Bay leaves, 2

MAKES ABOUT 2 QUARTS (2 L)

Position a rack in the upper third of the oven and preheat to 425°F (220°C). Spread all of the beef bones in a large roasting pan. Roast until the bones are nicely browned, about 40 minutes.

Just before the bones are ready, in a stockpot, heat the oil over medium-high heat. Add the onion, carrot, and celery and cook, stirring occasionally, until lightly browned, about 5 minutes. Transfer the browned bones to the stockpot. Pour out and discard the fat in the roasting pan. Place the roasting pan over high heat. Add 2 cups (16 fl oz/500 ml) cold water and bring to a boil, stirring with a wooden spoon to loosen any browned bits on the pan bottom. Pour the contents of the pan into the pot. Add cold water to cover the bones by 1 inch (2.5 cm). Bring to a boil over high heat, skimming off any foam that rises to the surface. Add the parsley, thyme, peppercorns, and bay leaves.

Reduce the heat to low and simmer, uncovered, until the stock is full-flavored, at least 3 hours or up to 5 hours. Remove and discard the bones. Strain the stock through a colander into a large bowl. Discard the solids in the colander. Let the stock stand for 5 minutes, then skim off the fat from the surface. Use immediately, or let cool, cover, and refrigerate for up to 3 days or freeze for up to 3 months.

CREAMY GRITS

Chicken Stock (page 212) or broth, 2 cups (16 fl oz/500 ml)

Whole milk, 1 cup (8 fl oz/250 ml)

Water, 1 cup (8 fl oz/250 ml)

Kosher salt, 1 teaspoon

Stone-ground white grits, 1 cup (5 oz/155 g)

Sharp Chedddar cheese, ½ cup (2 oz/60 g) grated

MAKES 4 SERVINGS

In a medium heavy-bottom saucepan, whisk the broth, milk, water, and salt together. Whisk in the grits and bring to a boil over medium heat, whisking frequently. Reduce the heat to medium-low and cover the saucepan. Simmer, whisking often, until the grits are very thick and tender, 45 to 55 minutes. Stir the Cheddar into the grits.

GREEN CHILE SAUCE

Anaheim chiles, 2 lb (1 kg) fresh

Canola oil, 4 tablespoons (2 fl oz/60 ml)

White onion, 1 cup (4 oz/125 g) diced

Garlic, 4 cloves, minced

Dried marjoram, 2 teaspoons

Ground cumin, 1 teaspoon

All-purpose flour, 3 tablespoons

Kosher salt

MAKES ABOUT 4½ CUPS (36 FL OZ/1.1 L)

Preheat the broiler. Arrange the chiles on a rimmed baking sheet and broil, turning occasionally, until blackened on all sides, about 12 minutes. Transfer the chiles to a bowl, cover tightly with plastic wrap, and let cool until easy to handle. Peel off the blackened skins. Discard the stems, seeds, and ribs, and chop the chiles.

In a large, heavy saucepan, combine 1 quart (1 l) water with the chopped chiles and bring to a boil over high heat. Meanwhile, in a frying pan, warm 2 tablespoons of the oil over medium heat. Add the onion and cook until translucent, about 3 minutes. Stir in the garlic, marjoram, and cumin and cook until fragrant, about 1 minute. Add the onion mixture to the saucepan with the chiles, reduce the heat to medium-low, and simmer, stirring occasionally, until the chiles are very tender and the cooking liquid is cloudy, about 20 minutes.

In a medium saucepan, warm the remaining 2 tablespoons oil over low heat. Add the flour and cook, whisking constantly, until the mixture is dark beige with a nutty aroma, about 3 minutes. Whisk in about 1½ cups (12 fl oz/375 ml) of the chile mixture, then return to the larger saucepan. Return to a simmer. Cook, stirring often, until no trace of raw flour flavor remains, about 15 minutes. Season with salt. If desired, in a blender, process the chile mixture in batches until smooth. The sauce can be cooled, covered, and refrigerated for up to 4 days or frozen for up to 2 months.

RÉMOULADE

Mayonnaise (page 216 or purchased), 1 cup (8 fl oz/250 ml)

Cornichons, 1 tablespoon minced

Nonpareil capers, 1 tablespoon, rinsed

Fresh flat-leaf parsley, 1 tablespoon minced

Fresh tarragon, 2 teaspoons minced

Spicy brown mustard, preferably Creole, 1 teaspoon

Anchovy paste, ½ teaspoon

Garlic, 1 small clove, minced

MAKES ABOUT 1 CUP (8 FL OZ/250 ML)

In a bowl, mix together all of the ingredients until well blended. Cover and refrigerate for 1 hour before serving. Use at once or refrigerate for up to 4 days.

PICO DE GALLO

Tomatoes, 2 large ripe, seeded and diced

Yellow onion, ½ cup (2½ oz/75 g) finely chopped

Fresh cilantro, 3 tablespoons minced

Fresh lime juice, 1 tablespoon

Jalapeño chile, ½, seeded and minced, or more to taste

Kosher salt

MAKES ABOUT 2½ CUPS (20 OZ/625 G)

In a nonreactive bowl, combine the tomatoes, onion, cilantro, lime juice, and jalapeño. Season with salt. Cover and let stand at room temperature for at least 30 minutes or up to 3 hours.

MARINARA SAUCE

Plum tomatoes with purée, preferably San Marzano, 2 cans (28 ounces/875 g each)

Olive oil, 3 tablespoons

Yellow onion, 1 large, finely diced

Garlic, 2–4 cloves, minced

Hearty red wine, ½ cup (4 fl oz/125 ml)

Red pepper flakes, ¼ teaspoon

Bay leaf, 1

Fresh basil, ¼ cup (⅓ oz/10 g) chopped

MAKES ABOUT 6 CUPS (48 FL OZ/1.5 L)

Pour the tomatoes and their purée into a large bowl. Using your hands, crush the tomatoes between your fingers.

In a large, heavy nonreactive saucepan, heat the oil over medium heat. Add the onion and cook, stirring occasionally, until tender, about 5 minutes. Stir in the garlic and cook until fragrant, about 1 minute.

Add the wine and bring to a boil. Add the crushed tomatoes, red pepper flakes, and bay leaf. Raise the heat to medium-high and bring to a boil, stirring frequently. Reduce the heat to low and simmer, stirring occasionally to prevent scorching and adding water if the sauce thickens too quickly, until the sauce has thickened, about 1½ hours. During the last 15 minutes of simmering, stir in the basil. Discard the bay leaf.

Use the sauce at once, or let cool, cover, and refrigerate for up to 4 days or freeze for up to 3 months.

BASIL PESTO

Garlic, 1 or 2 cloves

Pine nuts, ¼ cup (1 oz/40 g)

Fresh basil leaves, 2 cups (2 oz/60 g) packed

Extra-virgin olive oil, ½ cup (4 fl oz/125 ml)

Parmesan cheese, ½ cup (2 oz/60 g) freshly grated

Kosher salt and freshly ground pepper

MAKES ABOUT 1 CUP (8 OZ/250 G)

With a food processor running, drop the garlic through the feed tube and process until minced. Turn off the processor, add the pine nuts, and pulse a few times

to chop. Add the basil and pulse a few times to chop coarsely. Then, with the processor running, add the oil through the feed tube in a slow, steady steam and process until a smooth, moderately thick paste forms, stopping to scrape down the bowl as needed. Transfer to a bowl and stir in the Parmesan. Season to taste with salt and pepper.

Use the pesto at once, or transfer to a storage container, top with a thin layer of oil, cover tightly, and refrigerate for up to 1 week.

FOR KALE PESTO VARIATION:
Replace the basil with equal parts stemmed kale. slivered, blanched almonds also make a delicious replacement for the pine nuts.

FOR ARUGULA PESTO VARIATION:
Replace the basil with equal parts arugula, or use 1 part arugula, and 1 part fresh mint leaves.

FOR CILANTRO PESTO VARIATION:
Replace the basil with fresh cilantro and add 1 teaspoon grated lemon zest.

KETCHUP

Crushed plum tomatoes, 1 can (28 ounces/875 g)

Light corn syrup, ¼ cup (1.25 oz/40 g)

Cider vinegar, 3 tablespoons

Yellow onion, 2 tablespoons minced

Red bell pepper, 2 tablespoons minced

Garlic, 1 small clove, minced

Light brown sugar, 1 tablespoon firmly packed

Kosher salt, 1 teaspoon

Freshly ground pepper, ⅛ teaspoon

Ground allspice, pinch

Ground cloves, pinch

Celery seeds, pinch

Yellow mustard seeds, pinch

Bay leaf, ½

MAKES ABOUT 1½ CUPS (12 OZ/375 G)

At least 1 day before serving, combine all of the ingredients in a heavy saucepan over medium heat.

Bring to a boil, stirring. Reduce the heat to medium-low and cook at a brisk simmer, stirring frequently, until the mixture thickens and has reduced by half, about 1 hour.

Rub the ingredients through a medium-mesh sieve into a heatproof bowl, discarding any solids that are left in the sieve. Let cool completely. Transfer to a covered container and refrigerate overnight to allow the flavors to blend before using. Use at once or refrigerate for up to 2 weeks.

MAYONNAISE

Large egg, 1
Fresh lemon juice, 1 tablespoon
Dijon mustard, 1 teaspoon
Fine sea salt, ¼ teaspoon
Freshly ground white pepper, ⅛ teaspoon
Olive oil, ¾ cup (6 fl oz/180 ml)
Canola oil, ¾ cup (6 fl oz/180 ml)

MAKES ABOUT 1½ CUPS (12 FL OZ/375 ML)

Place the egg in a bowl, add hot tap water to cover, and let stand for 5 minutes to take the chill off. Crack the egg into a food processor. Add the lemon juice, mustard, salt, and white pepper. Combine the olive and canola oils in a glass measuring cup. With the processor running, add the oils through the feed tube in a slow, steady steam and process until the mayonnaise is thick. Add 1 tablespoon hot water and process briefly; the texture will become noticeably creamier. Taste and adjust the seasoning. Use at once, or cover and refrigerate for up to 5 days.

Return to the saucepan and bring to a boil over high heat. Reduce the heat to medium-low, and cook, stirring frequently, until reduced to about 2 cups (16 fl oz/ 500 ml), about 30 minutes. Season with salt and pepper. Cover and keep the sauce warm over very low heat.

PIZZA DOUGH

Active dry yeast, 1 envelope (2½ teaspoons)
Warm water (105°–115°F/40–46°C), ¼ cup (2 fl oz/60 ml)
Extra-virgin olive oil, ¼ cup (2 fl oz/60 ml), plus more for oiling
Fine sea salt, 1½ teaspoons
Sugar, 1 teaspoon
Bread flour, 3 cups (15 oz/465 g), or as needed

FOR TWO 12-INCH (30-CM) PIZZAS OR 6 CALZONES

At least 10 hours before making pizza or calzone, in a small bowl, sprinkle the yeast over the warm water and let stand until foamy, about 5 minutes. Transfer the yeast mixture to the bowl of a stand mixer fitted with the paddle attachment. Add 1 cup (8 fl oz/250 ml) cold water, the oil, the salt, and the sugar.

With the mixer on medium-low speed, add the flour to make a soft dough that does not stick to the sides of the bowl. Stop the mixer and cover the bowl with a kitchen towel, wrapping it around the paddle attachment. Let stand for 10 minutes.

Remove the towel and the paddle attachment and fit the stand mixer with the dough hook attachment. Knead the dough on medium speed, stopping the mixer and pulling the dough off the hook if it climbs up, until the dough is smooth and supple, about 8 minutes. Transfer the dough to a lightly floured work surface and knead by hand for 1 minute. Shape the dough into a taut ball. Lightly oil a large bowl. Add the dough, turn to coat it with the oil, and arrange smooth side up. Cover the bowl tightly with plastic wrap. Refrigerate until doubled in size, at least 8 or up to 36 hours. Remove the dough from the refrigerator 1–2 hours before rolling it out.

FOR HERB DOUGH VARIATION: Stir in about 2 tablespoons chopped fresh herbs or 1 tablespoon crumbled dried herbs into the dry ingredients. Use one or two of your favorite herbs, such as oregano, thyme, basil, rosemary, sage, fennel seed, marjoram, or chives.

BUTTERY PASTRY DOUGH

All-purpose flour, 1¼ cups (6½ oz/200 g)

Fine sea salt, ¼ teaspoon

Unsalted butter, 7 tablespoons (3½ oz/105 g), chilled

Ice water, ¼ cup (2 fl oz/60 ml), or as needed

MAKES ONE 9-INCH (23-CM) TART OR QUICHE

In a large bowl, whisk together the flour and salt. Cut the butter into cubes and scatter over the flour mixture. Using a pastry blender or 2 knives, cut the butter into the flour mixture until the mixture forms coarse crumbs the size of peas. Drizzle the ice water over the flour mixture and toss with a fork until the mixture forms moist clumps. If the dough seems too crumbly, add a little more ice water.

Form the dough into a disk (some flakes of butter should be visible), wrap in plastic wrap, and refrigerate for at least 30 minutes or up to 2 hours. Or, overwrap with aluminum foil and freeze for up to 1 month, then thaw in the refrigerator before using.

FLAKY PASTRY DOUGH

All-purpose flour, 1¼ cups (6.5 oz/220 g)

Sugar, 1 tablespoon (optional; see note)

Fine sea salt, ¼ teaspoon

Unsalted butter, 5 tablespoons (2.5 oz/75 g), chilled

Vegetable shortening, 2 tablespoons, chilled

Ice water, about ¼ cup (2 fl oz/60 ml)

FOR ONE 9-INCH (23-CM) PIE OR QUICHE

In a large bowl, whisk together the flour, sugar (if using), and salt. Cut the butter and shortening into chunks and scatter over the flour mixture. Using a pastry blender or 2 knives, cut the butter and shortening into the flour mixture just until the mixture forms large, coarse crumbs the size of peas.

Drizzle the ice water over the flour mixture and toss with a fork until the dough forms moist clumps. If the dough seems too crumbly, add a little more ice water.

Form the dough into a disk, wrap in plastic wrap, and refrigerate for at least 30 minutes or up to 2 hours.

Or, overwrap with aluminum foil and freeze for up to 1 month, then thaw in the refrigerator before using.

NOTE: Add the sugar if you are using the pastry dough for a dessert recipe and omit it if you are using it for a savory dish, such as quiche.

CHOCOLATE CURLS

Semisweet chocolate, about 6 ounces/185 g, in a single piece

MAKES ABOUT ½ CUP (2.5 OZ/75 G)

Heat the chocolate in a microwave on medium-low (30 percent) to soften just slightly, about 15 seconds. Using a vegetable peeler, shave curls from the chocolate onto a sheet of parchment paper. Refrigerate the curls to firm them slightly before using, about 10 minutes.

WHIPPED CREAM

Heavy cream, 1 cup (8 fl oz/250 ml)

Sugar, 2 tablespoons

Pure vanilla extract, ½ teaspoon

MAKES ABOUT 2 CUPS (16 OZ/500 G)

In a chilled bowl, combine the cream, sugar, and vanilla. Using a handheld mixer on medium-high speed, beat until soft peaks form. Use at once or cover and refrigerate for up to 2 hours before serving.

CHOCOLATE FROSTING

Confectioners' sugar, 3¾ cups (15 oz/470 g)

Unsweetened natural cocoa powder, 1 cup (3 oz/90g)

Unsalted butter, ½ cup (4 oz/125 g), at room temperature

Pure vanilla extract, 1 teaspoon

Heavy cream, about 1 cup (8 fl oz/250 ml)n

MAKES ABOUT 1½ CUPS (3 OZ/90 G)

In in a bowl, sift together the confectioners' sugar and cocoa. Using the mixer on low speed, mix in the butter until it is crumbly. Mix in the vanilla, and then gradually mix in enough of the cream to make a spreadable frosting. Use immediately.

INDEX

weldon**owen**

415 Jackson Street, 3rd Floor, San Francisco, CA 94111
www.weldonowen.com

COMFORT FOOD

Conceived and produced by Weldon Owen, Inc.
In collaboration with Williams-Sonoma, Inc.
3250 Van Ness Avenue, San Francisco, CA 94109

A WELDON OWEN PRODUCTION

Printed and bound in China by 1010 Printing, Ltd.

First printed in 2014
10 9 8 7 6 5 4 3 2 1

Library of Congress Cataloging-in-Publication
data is available.

ISBN 13: 978-1-61628-826-6
ISBN 10: 1-61628-826-4

Weldon Owen is a division of
BONNIER

WELDON OWEN, INC

CEO and President Terry Newell
VP, Sales and Marketing Amy Kaneko
VP, Publisher Roger Shaw

Associate Publisher Amy Marr
Associate Editor Emma Rudolph

Creative Director Kelly Booth
Art Director Alisha Petro
Senior Production Designer Rachel Lopez Metzger

Production Director Chris Hemesath
Associate Production Director Michelle Duggan

Photographers Peden+Munk
Food Stylist Alison Attenborough
Food Stylist Assistant Hadas Smirnoff
Kitchen Assistant Shelly Ellis
Prop Stylist Amy Wilson
Prop Stylist Assistant Nina Lalli

ACKNOWLEDGEMENTS

Weldon Owen wishes to thank the following people for their generous support in producing this book:
Devon Allred, Dawn Hill Antiques, Perry Fallon, Jane Fredrickson, Ernest Lupinacci, Del Martin,
Elizabeth Parson, John and Paulette Peden, Jodi Rappaport, and Aaron Sterling